70·HIKING TRAILS

**NORTHERN
OREGON
CASCADES**

DON AND ROBERTA LOWE

THE TOUCHSTONE PRESS
P.O. BOX 81
BEAVERTON, OREGON 97005

Library of Congress
Catalog Card No. 74-84378

I.S.B.N. No. 0-911518-29-0

Maps courtesy of
U.S. Geological Survey

INTRODUCTION

Residents of the Portland metropolitan area have some of the most scenic alpine terrain in Oregon practically in their backyards. Trailheads near the south side of Mt. Hood are only 1½ hours by car from downtown Portland and just half that time is needed to reach the hikes in the Columbia Gorge.

Even before automobiles and freeways, Portlanders were frequent visitors to Mt. Hood. Outdoor enthusiasts would take the train through the Columbia Gorge to Hood River and travel by stage to Cloud Cap on the north side of the peak. Those visiting Government Camp could hire four horse rigs from such firms as Hunter's Livery Stable on S.E. 34 Ave. or, after 1913, they could ride in one of the automobiles operated by the Reliance Mount Hood Stages.

Although recreationists have been enjoying the Mt. Hood area for over a century, hiking there has been popular only for the last fifty years. The first climbing group reached the summit of the peak in the 1850's; cycling to the Government Camp area enjoyed a burst of popularity during the 1890's; skiing was introduced in the first few years of the 1900's and not long after that motoring through the quagmires or dust bowls of the Barlow Road to Government Camp became a favorite adventure. However, when Paradise Park was visited by a group of Mazamas in 1922 this lovely spot was almost unknown. Similarly, the following year another party visited a second then unfamiliar site — Eden Park. By the early 1930's a "use path" had been worn from Cloud Cap to Eden Park, in 1938 the Timberline Trail around Mt. Hood near the 6,000 foot level was completed and since then the number of hikers who tromp over the more than 800 miles of trails in the Mt. Hood area has become substantial.

The first 21 hikes described in this guide are in the Columbia Gorge and the trailheads of all but the final three are reached from I 80N (the Columbia River Highway). Hikers already had been following trails in the Columbia Gorge for over a decade when the first camping groups visited Paradise and Eden Parks. Today, as then, one of the attractions of the Gorge is its low elevation. During late spring, while the high country around Mt. Hood is still snow covered, the hikes in the Columbia Gorge are at their best. Perky wild flowers brighten the slopes and earth smells waft through the air. The climb along Ruckle Creek Trail (No. 11) passes some flower displays particularly impressive in their variety and profusion. Similarly, when the first snows of winter have put an end to hiking above 3,500 feet, the trails in the Gorge still are open, except perhaps for the very highest sections of the longer ones. A characteristic shared by almost all the trails in the Gorge is the varied, always pleasing scenery. Since the destination of each trip is only the last of many attractions, you can end the hike wherever you wish and still have a satisfying outing. Another common characteristic is the considerable elevation gain. During late spring mountain climbers use this uphill to their advantage by taking the most demanding of the trails as conditioning hikes.

The last four hikes in this book actually visit areas slightly closer to Mt. Jefferson than to Mt. Hood. Their trailheads are reached along Oregon 224 (the Clackamas River Road). By establishing a base camp you can combine the trips to Pansy Basin and Bull of the Woods (No. 69) and Welcome Lakes (No. 70) into one excursion.

The remaining 45 hikes, numbers 22 through 66, are in the immediate vicinity of Mt. Hood and 13 of these trips (No's. 28, 29, 30, 32, 34, 37, 51, 52, 56, 57, 58, 59 and 63) travel along the slopes of the peak. Wild flowers are abundant in the immediate Mt. Hood area, particularly in the open areas. The region is noted especially for its rhododendrons that grow between 2,000 and 5,000 feet and bloom from late June through early July. Some of the plants offer more than good looks — huckleberry bushes are dense along a few of the trails and during August when their tempting fruit is ripe you may make very slow progress. Equally delicious, but more work to pick, are the wild blackberries and strawberries.

Some of the scree slopes are homes for conies and marmots, deer are plentiful and coyotes and bear also live in the woods but they seldom are seen. You can enjoy almost 40 miles of the best alpine scenery in northern Oregon by following the Timberline Trail (No. 59). Also, the northern most section of the Pacific Crest National Scenic Trail (Skyline) in Oregon from the Columbia River to Twin Lakes is described in No's. 13, 21, 23, 27, 59, 63 and 64.

HOW TO USE THIS BOOK

Preceding the body of the text for each trail is an information capsule listing seven important facts:

Hikes are recommended as one **day trip** or **backpack.** A one day trip usually is either very short or lacks suitable sites for camping. A trip classified as a one day trip or backpack (for which you carry overnight camping equipment) means the hike can be done in one day but because of the length, scenic attractions, possible side and loop trips or the availability of good campsites, you may prefer to take two or more days. Backpacks normally are too long or strenuous for the average hiker to make without a layover before returning.

Hiking **distance** is measured one way only, except for the few trips written as loops.

Since many hikes have a loss of altitude that is subsequently regained, **elevation gain** is listed as the total footage increment, not just the difference between the highest and lowest points. Significant elevation loss, if any, also is shown.

The **hiking time** is determined from the basic rate of two miles per hour plus allowance for rest stops, the steepness of the grade and the elevation gain. Trails are not graded according to difficulty, since this would necessitate a subjective evaluation that might not fit each individual's concept of an easy or hard hike. After a few trips you will be able to grade the trails for yourself by comparing the mileage and elevation gain, the major factors in determining how strenuous a hike will be, and by considering conditions such as the weather and how you feel on a specific day. Also, after a few hikes you will be able to predict whether your hiking speed is generally faster or slower than the times listed.

The **period when the trails are open** will vary each year depending upon the depth of the snowpack and the prevailing temperature. If you have doubts about a particular area, check with the ranger station nearest the trail or contact the Mt. Hood National Forest headquarters in Portland.

Since you may need to allow extra time to make a trip that travels at an elevation substantially higher than that to which you are acclimated, the **high point** for each hike is given.

The **U.S.G.S. topographic map(s) name, scale and date** are included because many of the side and loop trips suggested in the text are beyond the boundaries of the maps printed for each trail and you may want to purchase appropriate ones for the area not shown. In major cities U.S.G.S. topographic maps are sold through selected retail outlets or you can obtain them from the U.S. Government by sending $.75 and identifying information for each map to: Denver Distribution Section, U.S. Geological Survey, Federal Center, Denver, Colorado 80225.

The text for each trail is in three main sections: the first paragraph(s) describe special features of the hike such as good viewpoints, impressive wild flower displays and possible side or loop trips. The second part gives driving directions. Although some access roads to the trailheads are unpaved, these generally have good surfaces. The remainder of the text describes the trail route and includes comments on points of interest along the way and directions for any side or loop trips. Extreme steepness, lack of water, unmarked junctions, difficult fords and other problems you may encounter are noted. Where appropriate, the numbers of other trails in this guide are given in the text, such as some references to loops or side trips.

The maps for each trail are enlarged or reduced sections of topographic maps produced by the U.S. Geological Survey. The items in red are those that are particularly important in helping you find, stay on and enjoy the trail. A legend for these items can be found following the Table of Contents. The trail mileages shown may not always agree with those on trail signs. Map mileages are taken from known points or have been interpolated from specific fixes. Frequently, you will see trails on the topographic maps that are not overlayed in red. They either have no relevance to the trail being described or are no longer maintained. Campsites are marked with open triangles and may or may not be improved. Campgrounds reached by roads are marked with a solid triangle. Water is not necessarily available at the identified campsites, although mention usually is made in the text if the spot is "dry." Important sources of water not obvious from the topographic map are identified by the word "water."

Topographic maps are simple in theory and enable you to visualize the terrain covered by a trail. Through interpretation of these maps you can determine to some extent beforehand the difficulty of the trail and the feasibility of making a loop or reaching a point off the main route. Also, in case you become confused, being able to read a topographic map may make it easier for you to orient yourself.

The curvy lines on the topographic map are called contour lines and they connect points of equal elevation. The space between any two contour lines is termed a "contour interval" and is a measure of vertical distance. The closer the contour lines the steeper the terrain. How steep depends on the size of the contour interval which, in this book, is either 40 or 80 feet. You can calculate the interval for a map by finding the difference between any two consecutive figures appearing along every fifth contour line and then dividing by five. Keep the contour interval in mind when you study each map because terrain that appears steep on a map with 80 foot contour intervals is far steeper than terrain marked by 40 foot contour intervals spaced the same distance apart on a map of the same scale.

Unshaded areas on the topographic maps are regions of little or no vegetation. Original maps have a green overprint depicting areas with plant cover. In this book these appear as a medium to dark grey shade depending on the density of the green ink used in the original map. Figures along the contour lines, at the summits of peaks or elsewhere mark elevations above mean sea level. All maps in the book are north oriented.

Recreation maps prepared by the Forest Service are another good source of information, particularly for extended excursions. Although these maps show most of the latest trails and are an aid in planning side and loop trips, they do not show contour lines. These maps are available from the Mt. Hood National Forest headquarters, 2440 S.E. 195th, Portland, Oregon 97233, telephone 666-0511 or the regional office of the Forest Service, 319 S.W. Pine Portland, Oregon 97204, telephone 221-2877 or the district ranger stations. Incidentally, all the trails described in this guide are within the Mt. Hood National Forest. For a last minute source of information talk with ranger station personnel who have jurisdiction over the area you will be visiting. They often can tell you about new trail construction, road conditions and offer other helpful suggestions.

HIKING and BACKPACKING IN THE NORTHERN OREGON CASCADES

Hiking and backpacking techniques are not discussed here because many fine books are available that cover the subject thoroughly. However, a few points concerning outdoor travel in northern Oregon are reviewed.

Although most of the 70 hikes described in this guide can be done in tennis shoes, a good pair of hiking boots with lug soles will give you better traction and more foot support. (However, tennis shoes are good to include in your pack for fording streams or for camp wear.) If you are sensitive to the sun you may want to wear sun glasses, a wide brimmed hat and a long sleeved shirt.

The hiker in the Mt. Hood area encounters few of the problems found in many alpine areas: there are no daily lightning storms, no rattlesnakes, the elevation is not extreme, the weather is moderate and, with a few exceptions, streams usually are not swollen. However, accidents have occurred on even the smoothest trails and weather conditions can change quickly in any mountainous terrain so always include a wool hat, gloves, a sweater, a windbreaker and a poncho or some other water-proof garment in your pack. A flashlight, a first aid kit and food in addition to your lunch also should be standard equipment. Although mention is made in the text if no water is available along the trail, you should always fill your bottle before leaving home or camp.

Unfortunately, poison oak does exist in parts of the Columbia Gorge. Learn to recognize the plant. If you inadvertently come in contact with it or want to be extra careful, take a thorough shower when you return home and launder the outer clothing you wore. Ticks inhabit the Gorge, too, so immediately investigate any sensation of something crawling on you and check yourself carefully as soon as you return home to avoid tick bites. However, if one has bitten you but not burrowed in too far you, or a friend, can extract it with a *slow*, steady pull. Ticks are most common during spring, but a few stragglers remain all summer and into fall so observe the above precautions on all trips. Fortunately, the ticks in the Columbia Gorge are not known to transmit Rocky Mountain spotted fever.

Just because it rains in northern Oregon is no reason to cancel hikes. A large umbrella will keep your head, shoulders (and glasses, if you wear them) dry and you will not have to wear those ponchos that trap your body heat and get you more wet from the inside than you would from the inclement weather.

The authors hiked each of the trails in this book during 1972-73 to insure that the most accurate and up-to-date trail information was available. However, trails change or are changed, either because of rock fall, washouts and other natural causes, or because the officials who maintain the trails decide to establish alternate routes. It is the intention of the authors to revise this volume every five years. If you wish to assist in this updating process, you are invited to send changes or irregularities noted on your hikes to the authors in care of The Touchstone Press, P.O. Box 81, Beaverton, Oregon 97005.

.   By enjoying the many delights offered by hiking and backpacking you accept an obligation both to the wilderness you are visiting and to those who will follow. Therefore, your presence should leave the wilderness unchanged. By adhering to this ethic you will cause the least damage to the environment and the least offense to your fellow outdoorsmen.

Leave no litter (including lunch refuse) and *take* no wild flowers, plant life or other specimens. Also, do not disturb the animals you may be fortunate enough to see. Aural blight can be as disturbing to others as the visual variety: for instance, loud shouting; radios or noisy dogs can be very annoying to those who are trying to enjoy wild sounds.

Because their impact is greater, backpackers, especially, need to familiarize themselves with the proper techniques of locating and establishing campsites and the disposal of wastes.

D.L.
R.L.

contents

LEGEND

⬡	Starting Point
- - - -	Trail
· · · · · · · ·	Obscure Trail
△	Campsite
▲	Campground
■ ◣	Building or Remains
8.0	Mileage
No. 611	Trail No.
S42	Road No.
--✕--	Bridge
════	Access Road

AREA MAP

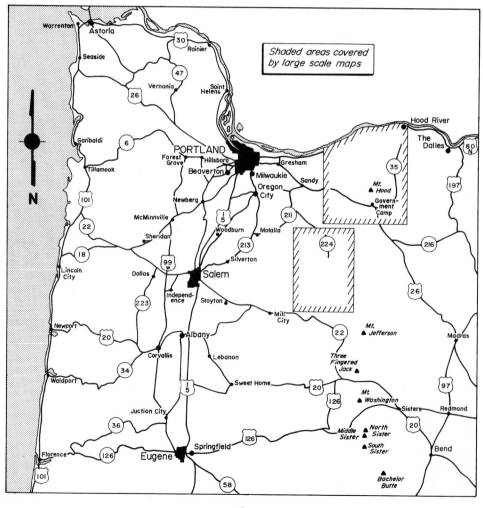

Shaded areas covered by large scale maps

AREA MAPS

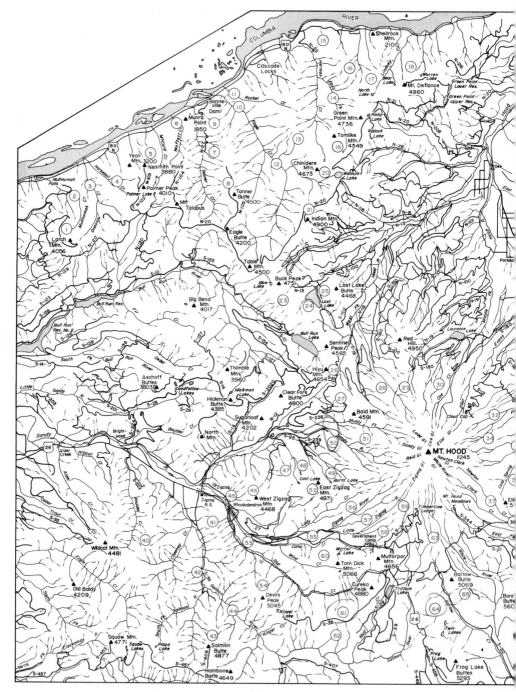

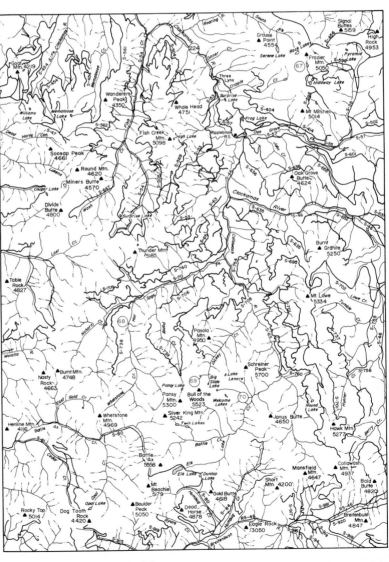

1 LARCH MOUNTAIN

One day trip or backpack
Distance: 7 miles one way
Elevation gain: 4,020 feet
High point: 4,075 feet
Allow 4 hours one way
Usually open May through November
Topographic map:
 U.S.G.S. Bridal Veil, Wash-Oreg.
 15'   1954

As you drive east from Portland, the outline of Larch Mountain is the first easily identified feature in the Columbia Gorge. Seen from a distance, the gradual, wooded slopes belie the varied scene of deep woods, rushing streams and many waterfalls the hiker passes during the climb to the summit. The two fords near 3.0 miles are a problem only early in the season and during periods of heavy runoff.

Because of the network of trails in the area you can return along one of several different routes. Since the hike ends at a paved road, you could do the trip one way only by establishing a long car shuttle. A considerably shorter car shuttle would be needed if you decided to descend along the Oneonta Creek Trail (No. 3) and none would be involved in returning along the Franklin Ridge Trail (No. 2). A considerably shorter hike that bypasses the summit of Larch Mountain is possible by taking No. 444 from the Larch Mountain Trail to the Franklin Ridge Trail.

Drive on I 80N (the Columbia River Highway) to the Multonomah Falls exit and parking area.

Walk under the railroad tracks and cross the Old Columbia River Scenic Highway to the Visitor Center. Wind up the wide paved path to the frequently photographed bridge spanning Multnomah Creek between the Upper and Lower Falls. At the east end curve left and climb along the paved trail in numerous well-graded switchbacks to a ridge crest. Wind down the opposite side for a short distance and where the paved trail curves sharply right to a viewpoint at the top of Upper Multnomah Falls keep left (straight) and descend to the small bridge across Multnomah Creek. One hundred feet from the

span come to the junction of the Perdition Trail to Wahkeena Falls and keep left.

Hike up beside Multnomah Creek and during one short stretch walk along the base of an undercut area of the rocky wall. Climb in a series of short switchbacks above a large falls then traverse to the junction of the Wahkeena Trail. Keep left and after 200 yards cross Multnomah Creek on a large bridge. Descend slightly then walk at a very moderate grade to the junction of the high water trail. Except in times of heavy runoff you can keep right and walk beside the creek. Rejoin the alternate route near the confluence of the West Fork of Multnomah Creek and after a short distance where the trail forks keep right. At the south edge of Multnomah Basin come to a road and the junction of the Franklin Ridge Trail.

Cross the road, continuing in the same direction you had been heading, and resume hiking along the trail at a gradual grade. At 3.0 miles cross the East Fork just before its confluence with Multnomah Creek. Make some very short switchbacks and soon ford Multnomah Creek. Switchback and climb through woods then traverse a large scree slope and at 4.5 miles pass the junction of the connector, No. 444, to the Franklin Ridge Trail. One-half mile farther come to the camp at Cold Spring. Just west of the camp meet a spur that goes from the Larch Mountain Road to a quarry. Cross the road and continue up through woods as indicated by the signs. The final two miles to the top climb along the crest of a broad, wooded ridge to the shelter cabin near the summit. For the best view, follow the short trail north to Sherrard Point on the rim of the steep north face of Larch Mountain.

Mt. Hood from the summit of Larch Mountain

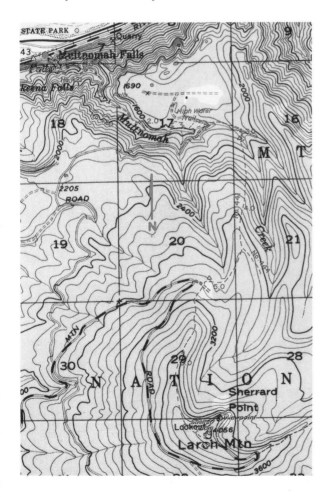

2 FRANKLIN RIDGE

One day trip or backpack
Distance: 10.6 miles one way
Elevation gain: 4,270 feet; loss 250 feet
High point: 4,075 feet
Allow 6 hours one way
Usually open May through November
Topographic map:
  U.S.G.S. Bridal Veil, Wash.-Oreg.
  15'   1954

The circuitous route of the Franklin Ridge Trail follows the Larch Mountain Trail beside Multnomah Creek for 2.5 miles then heads north across level Multnomah Basin before beginning the seven mile climb along the Ridge to the summit of Larch Mountain. Refer to Trail No. 1 for descriptions of the several possible loop trips.

Proceed on I 80N (the Columbia River Highway) to the Multnomah Falls exit and parking area.

Walk under the railroad tracks and cross the Old Columbia River Highway to the Visitor Center. Wind up the wide paved path, cross the bridge spanning Multnomah Creek between the Upper and Lower Falls and switchback up to a ridge crest. Wind down the opposite side and where the paved trail curves sharply right keep straight (left) and descend to the small bridge over Multnomah Creek. One hundred feet beyond the span come to the junction of the Perdition Trail to Wahkeena Falls and keep left. Hike parallel to Multnomah Creek, climbing in a series of short switchbacks along one stretch, to the junction of the Wahkeena Trail. Keep left and after 200 yards cross Multnomah Creek on a large bridge. Continue traversing to the junction of the high water trail. Unless the flow is heavy, keep right and walk along the water's edge. Rejoin the alternate route and after a short distance where the trail forks keep right. At the south edge of Multnomah Basin come to a road and the junction of the Larch Mountain Trail.

Keep left and continue along the road for 300 yards to a fork. Curve right and walk on the level for 200 yards to a path on your right. Follow this trail through deciduous woods to the road, turn right and after 150 feet turn left onto another shortcut. Walk for 0.1 mile to the same road, turn left and continue to its end at a turnaround.

Climb along a wide trail in the same direction you had been heading. At a fork keep right and continue traversing then drop slightly and come to a second branch. Turn right and begin climbing in a series of very short, moderately steep switchbacks. Rise at an even more severe grade then come to the crest in a grove of evergreens and travel on the level to a helispot at 4.0 miles. Although no water is available here, the impressive view makes it an ideal choice for a lunch stop. Continue along the crest that becomes broader and eventually begin traversing the west side of the slope below the ridge top, descending slightly during one section. At 5.8 miles come to the junction of the Oneonta Trail, No. 424 (No. 3).

Keep right then curve right and climb at a moderate grade along a broad crest. Traverse down the west side of the ridge for 200 feet then climb a short distance to another junction of the Oneonta Trail. Turn right onto No. 446, walk at a gradual grade then descend for a few hundred yards to a creek crossing. Climb moderately for a short distance to a crest then continue along the ridge top before descending to the junction of the Multnomah Creek Way Trail at 6.9 miles.

Turn left and soon pass a marsh on your right. Continue through woods then begin climbing considerably more steeply and make a few short switchbacks. Curve left and traverse in an easterly direction with slight ups and downs to an old railroad grade and turn left. Walk almost on the level for 0.5 mile, crossing several small side streams, to the junction of the Oneonta Trail. Turn right and climb along the ridge crest for 0.7 mile to the Larch Mountain Road. Walk up the road for ¼ mile to reach the parking area and the path to Sherrard Point.

Meadow below Larch Mountain

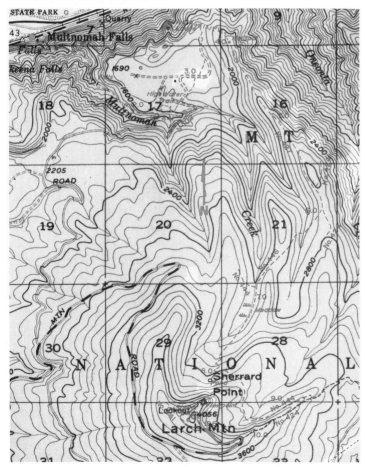

3 ONEONTA TRAIL

One day trip or backpack
Distance: 8 miles one way
Elevation gain: 4,225 feet; loss 200 feet
High point: 4,075 feet
Allow 5 hours one way
Usually open May through November
Topographic map:
 U.S.G.S. Bridal Veil, Wash.-Oreg.
 15'   1954

Like the trails along Multnomah and Eagle Creek Gorges (No's. 1 and 12), the route up the defile eroded by Oneonta Creek travels through woods of stately Douglas fir and delicate vine maple past many waterfalls ranging in character from the long, thin ethereal variety that seem to float down the walls to the considerably more voluminous ones formed by sudden drops in the stream bed. Midway along the hike the trail climbs over the rim of Oneonta Gorge and continues up through woods to the summit of Larch Mountain. Although difficult during periods of heavy runoff, the two fords of Oneonta Creek generally present few problems after the first part of July through early fall. Refer to the texts and maps of No's. 1 and 2 for possible loops.

Drive on I 80N (the Columbia River Highway) to the Ainsworth State Park-Warrendale exit located 4.0 miles east of the Multnomah Falls exit or 5.0 miles west of the Bonneville Dam interchange. From the exit drive west on the Old Columbia River Scenic Highway for two miles to a small sign on your left (south) side of the road stating Oneonta Trail. A large turnout is across the road.

Traverse up the wooded slope for 100 yards to an unsigned junction and keep straight (left). Switchback and continue climbing then cross over the face of a ridge and descend gradually to the junction of the trail from Horsetail Falls (No. 4). Keep straight (right) and traverse up the western wall of Oneonta Gorge at a generally moderate grade. Climb in one set of switchbacks then drop slightly to a view of Triple Falls. Continue downhill before resuming the climb and come to the first ford at 1.7 miles. After the crossing turn right and traverse for three-quarters mile, making two separate sets of switchbacks, and come to the second ford. The trail makes a short switchback from the west bank and climbs for 0.1 mile to meet

Horsetail Creek Trail (No. 4).

Keep straight (right) and after about 100 feet switchback right and begin the mile long climb up the southwestern wall of Oneonta Gorge. Just below the crest begin traveling through a swath of standing, dead trees then drop for a short distance to the junction of the Franklin Ridge Trail, No. 427 (No. 2). Turn left, traverse then soon curve right and climb at a moderate grade along a broad crest. Traverse down the west side of the ridge for 200 feet then climb a short distance to another junction.

Keep left (straight), climb over a small crest then descend and travel at a gradual grade before dropping again to a stream crossing. Climb, then go downhill to a second ford. Rise considerably more steeply, make five short switchbacks and about 200 feet beyond the last turn come to the junction of unidentified Bell Creek Way. Turn right and traverse at a moderate, but irregular, grade. Cross a small stream, descend briefly then walk on the level to a road. You are now in the Bull Run Reserve so stay on the authorized route for the next 0.5 mile.

Turn right and walk along the road for 250 yards to a sign on your left marking the resumption of the Oneonta Trail. Turn left and soon begin climbing along a ridge crest. Come to an old railroad grade and continue along it for 100 feet to the junction of No. 444 to the Franklin Ridge Trail. A railroad was used to log the area and several old ties can be seen imbedded in the Oneonta Trail just before the junction. Keep left (straight) and continue uphill for three-quarters mile to the Larch Mountain Road. Turn right and walk ¼ mile to the parking area and the path to Sherrard Point.

Along the Oneonta Creek Trail

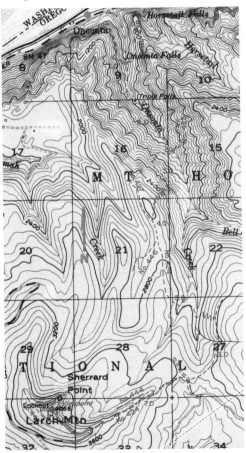

4 HORSETAIL CREEK TRAIL

One day trip
Distance: 9 miles one way
Elevation gain: 4,135 feet; loss 300 feet
High point: 3,880 feet
Allow 5½ to 6 hours one way
Usually open June through November
Topographic map:
U.S.G.S. Bridal Veil, Wash.-Oreg.
15'   1954

After traversing the steep walls of narrow Oneonta Gorge, the Horsetail Creek Trail turns east and climbs over the shoulder of Yeon Mountain to Nesmith Point. Since a second trail (No. 5) goes to the same destination, by establishing a short car shuttle you can enjoy new scenery and four fewer miles by returning along the more easterly route (Nesmith Point Trail). Although somewhat difficult during periods of heavy runoff, the three fords of Oneonta Creek generally present few problems after the first part of July through early fall.

Proceed on I 80N (the Columbia River Highway) to the Ainsworth State Park-Warrendale interchange located 4.0 miles east of the Multnomah Falls exit or 5.0 miles west of the Bonneville Dam interchange. From the exit drive west on the Old Columbia River Scenic Highway for 1.4 miles to a sign on your left (south) at Lower Horsetail Falls marking the beginning of the Horsetail Falls Trail. Many parking spaces are available on both sides of the road.

Climb moderately in several short switchbacks then traverse into a small side canyon and walk behind Upper Horsetail Falls. Leave the side canyon and traverse the face of the slope, dropping slightly. Where the trail forks you either can stay left on the main route or follow the right loop that passes a viewpoint. Hike along the wall of Oneonta Gorge then descend in short switchbacks to the large bridge over the creek. Climb in one set of switchbacks to the junction of the Oneonta Trail (No. 3) and turn left.

Traverse moderately up the western wall of Oneonta Gorge, make one set of switchbacks then drop slightly to a view of Triple Falls. Continue downhill before resuming the climb and come to the first ford at 1.7 miles. After the crossing turn right, traverse

for three-quarters mile, making two separate sets of short switchbacks, and come to the second ford. The trail makes a short switchback from the west bank and climbs for 0.1 mile to the junction of the Oneonta Trail.

Turn left and drop to the third ford. After the crossing climb steeply in a downstream direction for a couple hundred feet then switchback right and continue rising steeply. Begin traveling at a moderate grade, cross a small side stream then traverse through a slightly marshy and brushy area. Cross a second side stream and continue along the wooded slope. At 3.5 miles begin a series of many short switchbacks to the crest of the ridge then walk along the gradually inclined terrain in a southeasterly direction to the junction of Bell Creek Way at 5.0 miles.

Turn left, soon begin descending and come to the first of three crossings of the forks of Horsetail Creek. During the next 0.5 mile climb irregularly and ford the other two branches. Beyond the last crossing the trail becomes faint for a short distance. Climb more noticeably and come to the junction of the Mystery Trail, an unofficial semi-climbing route that starts below St. Peters Dome. Keep straight (right) and walk for 0.3 mile along the rim of the steep south wall of the Gorge then hike over the shoulder of Yeon Mountain. Continue gradually uphill to an overlook at 7.9 miles directly across from Beacon Rock and Hamilton Mountain.

Veer away from the rim and drop slightly to Road N122. Turn left and walk up the road, passing the sign marking the route of the Nesmith Point Trail after 0.2 miles. (On your return you will follow this route if you are making the recommended loop.) Continue climbing along the road then near the crest curve right and follow a path for several yards to the rocky site of the former lookout cabin.

Triple Falls

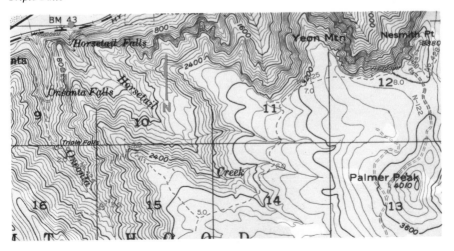

5 NESMITH POINT

One day trip
Distance: 5 miles one way
Elevation gain: 3,810 feet
High point: 3,880 feet
Allow 3 to 3½ hours one way
Usually open June through November
Topographic maps:
  U.S.G.S. Bonneville Dam, Oreg.-Wash.
  15'   1957
  U.S.G.S. Bridal Veil, Wash.-Oreg.
  15'   1954

Nesmith Point is one of the highest spots on the rim of the Columbia Gorge and from a viewpoint near the summit you look 3,750 feet down to Beacon Rock and across to Hamilton and Table Mountains. The trail to the Point was not maintained for many years and it became impassable but in 1972 the route was brushed out and rebuilt where necessary, so hikers once again can enjoy the varied terrain and extensive views along the circuitous route. Carry water as sources along the trail are not dependable.

You can make a loop trip by returning along the Horsetail Creek Trail (No. 4). This strenuous, but fun, circuit would add 3.5 miles of downhill hiking, involve three fords of Oneonta Creek and necessitate a short car shuttle.

From the west drive on I 80N (the Columbia River Highway) to the Ainsworth State Park-Warrendale exit located 4.0 miles east of the Multnomah Falls exit. After leaving the freeway turn left then 0.2 mile farther continue following the sign to Dodson and Warrendale and drive east, paralleling the highway, for two miles to the large parking area for Yeon State Park on your right just before the frontage road joins the freeway. From the east proceed 2.6 miles west of the Bonneville Dam interchange to the Warrendale exit. Drive below and parallel to the freeway for 0.4 mile then turn left and go under the highway. Turn left and proceed 0.3 mile to the parking area. The hike begins at the southwest edge of the turnout and is marked by a sign stating Elowah Falls Trail.

Climb a few yards along the bank then switchback left at an old, wooden water tank and 150 feet farther come to the signed junction of the Nesmith Point Trail. Turn right and travel at a gradual grade then curve left onto an old road bed for several yards. Travel along the wooded slope in an easterly direction then switchback right and head generally to the west. Pass an underground stream then begin traversing and cross a small scree slope. Switchback left just before coming to a stream that may not flow above ground all summer and recross the scree slope. Make one set of very short switchbacks to the ridge crest at 1.1 miles where a path leads left to a viewpoint.

Curve right and traverse at a more noticeable grade along the western wall of a small basin. Cross to the eastern side then return to the western slope and switchback up a narrow draw. Head west along the face of a vertical slope then climb in a second series of short switchbacks. Traverse for a short distance to the crest of a ridge, curve right and hike along the open wall of the huge upper basin. Cross to the eastern side in a long traverse then climb in several switchbacks to the rim of the basin at 3.0 miles where you can look down into McCord Creek canyon.

Curve right and traverse up the wooded slope for 0.4 mile then veer right and travel at a gradual grade. Walk slightly downhill for a short distance then resume a gradual to moderate climb. Pass through two small, open areas and come to a sign where the trail curves sharply right. If you are making the loop and want to save 300 feet of climbing and 0.7 mile you can bypass Nesmith Point by keeping straight (left) here and following the faint trail for 0.1 mile to Road N122. Turn right, walk up the road for 200 yards to the new sign marking Horsetail Creek Way and turn left.

To continue the climb to Nesmith Point curve right on the main trail and climb a short distance to N122. Turn right and wind up along the road for one-quarter mile. Near the edge of the rim curve right and follow a path for several yards to the rocky site of the former lookout cabin.

Nesmith Point from Hamilton Mountain

21

6 MUNRA POINT

One-half day trip
Distance: 1.3 miles one way
Elevation gain: 1,760 feet
High point: 1,850 feet
Allow 1½ hours one way
Usually open March through December
Topographic map:
   U.S.G.S. Bonneville Dam, Oreg.-Wash.
   15'   **1957**

Munra Point is the rocky, narrow high point of the steep ridge between Moffett and Tanner Creeks just southwest of Bonneville Dam. The landmark was named in 1915 for "Grandma" Munra who operated a railroad restaurant at Bonneville. The scene from the long crest includes the wooded slopes of Tanner Ridge, Moffett and Tanner Creek canyons, Table Mountain across the Columbia River and an aerial-like view down onto Bonneville Dam. In early April several varieties of wild flowers thrive along the grassy slopes at the southern end of the ridge.

Since the path to the crest climbs almost 2,000 feet in 1.3 miles, this is a good choice for a short, strenuous hike. However, the trail surface becomes slippery and dangerous during periods of wet weather, so the climb is best made after a dry spell. Many people carry ice axes or hiking canes to aid

in the descent. Start the trip with a full bottle of water as none is available along the climb.

From the west proceed on I 80N (the Columbia River Highway) to the Bonneville Dam exit. Go under the highway, turn left, reenter the freeway and head west 1.2 miles to a small sign identifying Moffett Creek. Leave the freeway from the left lane and drive into the flat, open area along the west side of the creek canyon. After the hike those whose destination is to the east will need to drive west along the freeway 1.4 miles to the Warrandale entrance to the freeway.

Walk east across the bridge and go under the raised east-bound lanes of the freeway then bear slightly left and follow an obvious path into the woods. Wind up along the forested slope to a ridge crest. Initially, the trail travels at a moderate grade, but it soon becomes steep and rocky. Head in a southerly direction and where a faint path heads upslope stay on the main route. Several yards farther switchback to the left and begin climbing very steeply. The grade becomes even more severe as you leave the deep coniferous woods and enter a zone of small oak trees. At a crest a side path goes left for a few yards to a viewpoint and the main trail turns right and climbs along the rocky, open crest. Several yards beyond the fork be watching for a path on your right that goes downslope. This is an alternate route that offers better footing and avoids the steepest part of the climb and is the preferable route to follow on the descent.

Veer south off the crest then return to the ridge top and climb for a short distance to a low rock outcropping. Although the scramble up its face is not difficult, on the return you may want to circumvent the obstacle by descending around its southern edge. Continue up the crest through evergreen woods and come to a high point where you can see the top of Munra Ridge. Veer right, make two short dips then go to your left along the base of a low, steep slope for several yards. Switchback right and climb along the upper section of the face. Traverse at a gradual grade along a grassy slope below the summit for 300 yards then climb a short distance to the ridge top.

To reach the viewpoint above Bonneville Dam, turn left (north) and follow the faint path along the western slope below the crest. A pleasant place to end the trip is to the south along the broader section of the summit ridge. Turn right at the crest and traverse along a slope of grass and wild flowers.

Munra Point and Table Mountain

7 DUBLIN LAKE

One day trip
Distance: 4 miles one way
Elevation gain: 2,580 feet; loss 220 feet
High point: 3,730 feet
Allow 2½ hours one way
Usually open late May through November
Topographic map:
  U.S.G.S. Bonneville Dam, Oreg.-Wash.
  15'   1957

The Columbia Gorge contains few lakes and several of those that do exist can not be reached by trail. Of the four in the Gorge visited by hikes described in this guide, tree-rimmed Dublin Lake is the most westerly and smallest. The hike crosses the Tanner Butte Trail (No. 8) at 3.5 miles and since you drive past the trailhead for the latter, you could establish a car shuttle and do the hike as a loop that would add about one mile of downhill. Also, on the optional return you could make a three-quarters mile side trip to the impressive overlook above Bonneville Dam on narrow, rocky Wauna Point (No. 9).

Follow I 80N (the Columbia River Highway) to the Bonneville Dam interchange. If you are approaching from the west turn right at the end of the exit and travel several yards to unpaved Tanner Creek Road. (From the east, turn left at the end of the exit and go under the freeway.) Turn left onto the road and go uphill, paralleling the freeway. After 0.5 mile curve right, pass a water tank and a sign stating Road N27. Drive along the road for 5.1 miles, passing the trailhead for the Tanner Butte-Wauna Point Trails after 1.1 miles, to where the gravel surface ends and the dirt road goes steeply downhill. Parking for several cars is available here.

(Note: As of June 1974, Forest Service personnel were considering closing the Tanner Creek Road to vehicular travel.)

Walk down the dirt road for several yards to a cement sign on your left stating Mountain Goat Trail, Tanner Butte Trail 4. Turn left and hike for 100 yards at a gradual grade through a wooded area densely carpeted with sorrel and, during mid-spring, the blossoms of bleeding heart and trillium. Cross a small stream and wind up through woods of wide-ly-spaced trees. Curve left and recross the stream you forded near the beginning of the hike. This is the last source of water. Begin rising more steeply then climb in a series of short switchbacks near the edge of a scree slope. The pyramid shape of Mt. Talapus in the Bull Run Reserve can be seen to the southwest. After a long traverse resume switchbacking at a moderately steep grade. The small, speckled pink blossoms of calyp-so orchids are abundant along this stretch. Come to the face of a ridge and wind steeply up to a crest and continue climbing. At 2.6 miles begin traversing to the east at an in-creasingly gradual grade until you are travel-ing almost on the level. At 3.5 miles meet the junction of the Tanner Creek Trail. If you make the loop on the return you will head north along the route to the left.

Turn right and climb gradually for 120 yards to an unsigned trail going to the left at a sitting log. Turn left, walk 100 feet before descending moderately for another 100 feet then drop steeply for several hundred yards to the northwest end of the lake.

24

Aerial view of Dublin Lake and the Columbia River

8 TANNER BUTTE

One day trip
Distance: 7.5 miles one way
Elevation gain: 3,550 feet; loss 150 feet
High point: 4,500 feet
Allow 5 to 6 hours one way
Usually open mid-June through November
Topographic map:
  U.S.G.S. Bonneville Dam, Oreg.-Wash.
  15'   1957

Massive Tanner Butte is situated in a remote, central area of the Columbia Gorge and because of its height and location landmarks on the Oregon side of the Gorge between Larch Mountain to the west and Chinidere Mountain to the east can be identified in addition to views of the major peaks in southern Washington and Mt. Hood. The climb is long and strenuous, a good choice for hikers or climbers wanting a demanding trip.

Follow I 80N (the Columbia River Highway) to the Bonneville Dam interchange. If you are approaching from the west turn right at the end of the exit and travel several yards to unpaved Tanner Creek Road. (From the east, turn left at the end of the exit and go under the freeway.) Turn left onto the road and go uphill, paralleling the freeway. After 0.5 mile curve right, pass a water tank and a sign stating Road N27. Continue 1.1 miles to the east end of a side canyon where a cement marker and a wooden sign identify the beginning of the Tanner Butte Trail. A turnout beside the road provides parking spaces for only a few cars.

(Note: As of June, 1974, Forest Service personnel were considering closing the Tanner Creek Road to vehicular traffic.)

Walk on the level for several yards then wind up above the north side of a creek in very short, steep switchbacks. Cross a small stream and traverse at a gradual grade into the canyon formed by the main flow. Make an easy ford and traverse out of the ravine along the south wall. Leave the woods and enter the open swath below the power lines. Walk around the face of the slope below the tower and continue traversing through the cleared area for a few hundred feet to a service road. Hamilton and Table Mountains are the prominent peaks rising above the Columbia River on the Washington side of the Gorge, Munra Point (No. 6) is the steep, grassy ridge across the valley to the west and Mt. Talapus in the Bull Run Reserve is the pyramid shaped peak to the south.

Cross the road to the resumption of the trail and traverse through a clearcut for 150 yards then reenter woods and climb at a steady, moderate grade. At 0.5 mile begin a set of long switchbacks then make a short switchback and at 1.0 mile walk around the face of a ridge. Traverse the east side of the slope then switchback and recross the crest. Soon climb in a series of short switchbacks then begin a long traverse across the western wall of a large, wooded basin. Pass a little side stream that may not flow all year and one-quarter mile farther come to a small bench where an unmarked path on your left descends for three-quarters mile to Wauna Point (No. 9).

Keep right and continue climbing along the wide, wooded ridge crest for 2.3 miles. At 4.6 miles pass the unsigned junction on your right of Trail No. 448 (No. 7) that begins farther south along Road N27. After 120 yards pass a second unsigned path that descends to the left for 0.2 mile to Dublin Lake. Continue straight on the main trail for 0.1 mile to an old road. Turn left and walk up the road at a gradual grade through less dense timber along the west side of the ridge for 1.5 miles then drop slightly to a saddle where you can see the northwestern slope leading to the summit of Tanner Butte.

Continue to the south end of the saddle then turn left and begin climbing cross-country near the northern edge of the slope. Although the final 0.4 mile and 500 feet of elevation gain are over trailless terrain, the going is not difficult and the correct route is obvious. On the summit a few remains are the only evidence of the fire lookout cabin that once stood here.

Mt. Hood from Tanner Butte

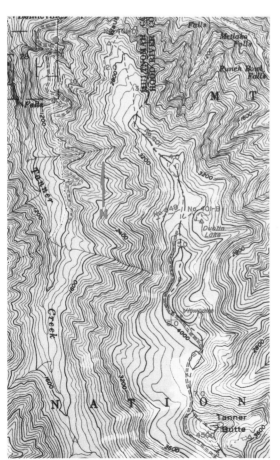

9 WAUNA POINT

One day trip
Distance: 3 miles one way
Elevation gain: 1,550 feet; loss 650 feet
High point: 2,650 feet
Allow 2 hours one way
Usually open April through November
Topographic map:
  U.S.G.S. Bonneville Dam, Oreg.-Wash.
  15'   1957

The view from the aery setting of Wauna Point is one of the most interesting in the Columbia Gorge so you probably will want to allow extra time for enjoying it. The vista extends west up the Gorge to Crown Point, east to beyond the Bridge of the Gods and north to Mt. Adams, Becon Rock and Table and Hamilton Mountains in Washington but most intriguing is the view 2,500 feet down onto Bonneville Dam and the ship locks. Follow I 8 on (the Columbia River Highway) to the Bonneville Dam interchange. If you are approaching from the west turn right at the end of the exit and travel several yards to unpaved Tanner Creek Road. (From the east turn left at the end of the exit and go under the freeway.) Turn left onto the road and go uphill, paralleling the freeway. After 0.5 mile curve right, pass a water tank and a sign stating Road N27. Continue 1.1 miles to the east end of a side canyon where a cement marker and a wooden sign identify the beginning of the Tanner Butte Trail. Parking space is limited.

(Note: As of June, 1974, Forest Service personnel were considering closing the Tanner Creek Road to vehicular traffic.)

Walk on the level for several yards then wind up above the north side of a creek in very short, steep switchbacks. Cross a small stream and traverse at a very moderate grade into the canyon formed by the main flow, the last dependable source of water. Make an easy ford and traverse out of the ravine along the south wall. Leave the woods and enter the open swath below the power lines. Walk around the face of the slope below the tower and continue traversing through the cleared area for a few hundred feet to a service road. Mt. Talapus in the Bull Run Reserve is the pyramid-shaped peak to the south. Talapus and Wauna are of Indian origin, the first being the word for coyote and the second the name of the mythological character who represented the Columbia River.

Cross the road to the resumption of the trail and traverse through a clearcut for 150 yards then reenter woods and climb at a steady, moderate grade. At 0.5 mile begin a set of long switchbacks then make a short switchback and at 1.0 mile walk around the face of a ridge. Traverse the east side of the slope then switchback and recross the crest. Soon climb in a series of short switchbacks and begin a long traverse across the western wall of a large, wooded basin. Pass a little side stream that may not flow all year and one-quarter mile farther come to a small bench where an unmarked path heads off to the left. The main route continues to Tanner Butte (No. 8).

Turn left and follow the sometimes faint, very moderately graded trail through woods and after 0.2 mile be watching for a path heading downhill in a slightly more open area. A small log blocks the path that continues straight here. Turn left and descend for 50 yards to a little stream and switchback right then traverse through woods along a narrow trail. (If you miss the turn and accidentally follow the path along the ridge crest, turn left where the tread stops and the slope ahead becomes very steep and descend cross-country for 75 yards to the main route. The angle of the slope is severe but the footing is good.) Begin winding down the east side of a narrow ridge crest in very short, steep switchbacks then walk along or near the crest. Where the route seems to fork, keep left and traverse along a semi-open, rocky slope. After 90 yards come to a crest and begin descending through woods. Drop for 75 yards, cross a very narrow, rocky portion of the ridge top then wind down the final 50 yards to Wauna Point. Return along the same route you followed down.

28

Table Mountain from the Wauna Point trail

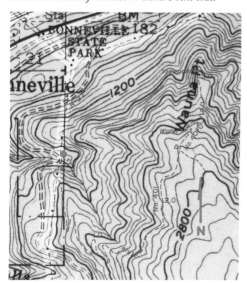

Falls near trail head

10 RUCKEL RIDGE

One day trip
Distance: 3.8 miles one way
Elevation gain: 3,700 feet; loss 100 feet
High point: 3,700 feet
Allow 3½ to 4 hours one way
Usually open June through November
Topographic map:
   U.S.G.S. Bonneville Dam, Oreg.-Wash.
   15'   1957

The climb of narrow, rocky Ruckel Ridge that forms the northern wall of Eagle Creek Canyon is one of the most strenuous trips in the Columbia Gorge. Its many viewpoints and varied scenes of deep woods and semi-open slopes of grass, oaks and wild flowers make it also one of the most enjoyable visually. You can do a superb loop trip by returning along the equally impressive Ruckel Creek Trail (No. 11). The circuit involves no extra mileage and the descent is easier. Carry water as none is available until the 3.8 mile point on the Benson Plateau.

From the west proceed on I 80N (the Columbia River Highway) to the Eagle Creek exit 1.2 miles east of the Bonneville Dam interchange. (After the hike you will have to continue east on the freeway two miles to reach the interchange at Cascade Locks.) If you are approaching from the east drive to the Bonneville Dam interchange and go east as described above. Leave your car in the large parking area just east of the fish hatchery buildings.

Walk north up the paved road for 100 yards to a sign on your left identifying the Buck Point Trail. Turn left and wind up through woods then walk beside a wire fence above the freeway. Where you come to the edge of the campground veer right through a camping unit to the loop road and turn left. Walk along the road to the southeast edge of the campground and unit number 6. The trail traverses south along the slope above this camping area then climbs in gradual, short switchbacks. About 0.2 mile from the campground be watching for an unsigned junction on your left by two large rocks several hundred yards before the main trail ends.

Turn left and after a brief moderate stretch begin climbing in very short, steep switchbacks. Come to an open area and climb to a viewpoint at a power transmission tower. Re-enter woods and descend slightly to a scree slope. A faint path traverses the rocks for about 60 yards then climbs steeply to the left for several yards. Where the obvious route stops, continue up over the rocks, veering slightly left, toward the west end of the short treeless ridge that extends for about 200 feet from the base of the cliff face. Turn right where you reach the ridge and climb along its crest to the base of the wall. Turn sharply left and follow the well-worn path along the base of the wall. Turn right, zigzag extremely steeply for 50 yards then continue uphill at a more moderate grade to the crest.

The next 1.5 miles generally follows up along the ridge top with a few short descents offering respites. One extremely narrow, exposed section can be circumvented by dropping to the right. At 2.6 miles, a short distance beyond the knife-edge ridge, come to an open slope of knobby rocks.

Follow the faint path to the right around the south face of the slope, enter woods where the path soon stops and wind down for about 100 feet to a saddle. Scramble up the north (left) side of the ridge to the crest where the trail resumes. The grade initially is moderate but becomes increasingly steeper and near the end of the ridge the trail is faint. Where you reach the almost level area that marks the edge of the plateau turn left and follow the blazes for several hundred yards to Ruckel Creek.

If you are making the loop, ford the stream and climb gradually to the left at a 35° angle to the flow until you intersect Ruckel Creek Way. Turn left and begin descending.

Trail above the first cliffs

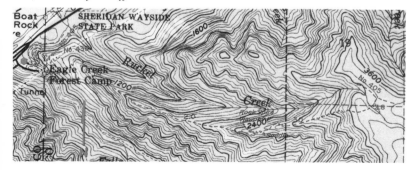

11 RUCKEL CREEK

One day trip
Distance: 4 miles one way
Elevation gain: 3,600 feet
High point: 3,700 feet
Allow 3 to 3½ hours one way
Usually open May through November
Topographic map:
   U.S.G.S. Bonneville Dam, Oreg.-Wash.
   15'   1957

This scenic, but strenuous, hike is best done in May when the two large hanging meadows midway along the climb are filled with the vivid blossoms of assorted wild flowers. In addition to these grassy areas, the route passes through attractive woods, a vast rocky area with several Indian pits and a viewpoint at the edge of a 600-foot high cliff. A superb loop trip can be made by climbing along Ruckel Ridge (No. 10) to the edge of the Benson Plateau and returning on the Ruckel Creek Trail.

From the west drive on I 80N (the Columbia River Highway) 1.2 miles east of the Bonneville Dam interchange to the Eagle Creek exit. (After the hike you will have to continue east on the freeway two miles to reach the interchange at Cascade Locks.) If you are approaching from the east drive to the Bonneville Dam interchange and go east as described above. Leave your car in the large parking area just east of the fish hatchery buildings.

Walk to the north up the paved road for 100 yards to a sign on your left identifying the Buck Point Trail. Turn left and wind up through woods above the fish hatchery then walk beside a wire fence above the freeway for 50 yards to the northeast edge of the campground where a sign by a wooden fence identifies the beginning of the Ruckel Creek Trail.

Keep left and descend to a large, flat open area. Walk through the clearing, aiming for the southeast side then curve right and meet a section of the Old Columbia River Highway roadbed. Turn left and follow the road to a small, ornate bridge over Ruckel Creek. At the east end of the span turn right onto a trail, pass a sign and hike uphill beside the stream, the last dependable source of water until the end of the hike. Fifty yards from the old roadbed switchback left and begin climbing through woods. Enter a narrow cleared area at 0.7 mile and cross under power lines then resume climbing steeply through the scenic forest. Come to the edge of a massive, rocky slope, drop slightly and wind across it. Near the eastern end pass some Indian pits on your right. Although several explanations have been offered, anthropologists are not certain of the role these depressions played in Indian culture.

Resume climbing through woods, enter a rocky gully and one-half mile from the pits come to an aery viewpoint where you will be able to see down to Cascade Locks, the Columbia River and Bonneville Dam. Reenter deep woods, climb in short switchbacks and drop along a grassy, more open slope to the first of the two large hanging meadows. After passing through the second meadow traverse through woods and climb in several short switchbacks. Drop into a little gully and cross the face of a steep slope. The trail is rough here for several yards but the tread is obvious. Beyond the face curve left and resume traversing. At 3.0 miles begin to wind steeply up through woods then hike across a small scree slope, switchback a few times and traverse into deeper woods. If you want to end the hike in the woods beside Ruckel Creek continue to a sign then leave the trail and head downhill toward the stream at a 35° angle, reaching the bank after about 150 yards. The flow originally was called Deadman Creek but the name was changed to commemorate J. S. Ruckel who in 1861 built the portage tramway on the Oregon side of the Columbia River at the Cascades.

Upper portion of Ruckel Creek trail

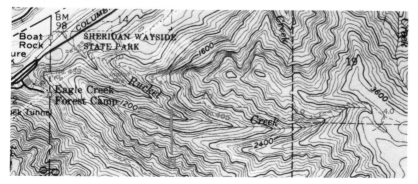

√12 EAGLE CREEK TRAIL

Backpack
Distance: 14 miles one way
Elevation gain: 3,840 feet
High point: 3,950 feet
Allow 8 to 10 hours one way
Usually open June through November
Topographic map:
  U.S.G.S. Bonneville Dam, Oreg.-Wash.
  15'   1957

The popular trail along the Eagle Creek Gorge is considered by many hikers to be the most scenic trip in the Columbia Gorge. This evaluation is related to a succession of high waterfalls along both sides of the canyon and on Eagle Creek itself, sheer rock walls, deep defiles spanned by high bridges, and attractions such as the much photographed Punchbowl and the 25-foot long tunnel carved behind, appropriately named, Tunnel Falls. The moderate climb to a level spot beside Eagle Creek at 6.5 miles make an ideal destination for a one day trip. Refer to No. 13 for a description of the two possible loops and to No. 21 for driving directions to Road N20 if you want to do the hike one way only. Due to the exposure along portions of the hike, this is not a suitable trip for very young children.

Proceed on I 80N 1.2 miles east of the Bonneville Dam interchange to the Eagle Creek exit. (After the hike you will have to continue east on the freeway two miles to reach the interchange at Cascade Locks if your destination is to the west.) Where the road forks just beyond the east end of the fish hatchery buildings keep right and drive 0.5 mile along the narrow, level dirt road to its end at a large turnaround. A sign listing several mileages marks the beginning of the trail.

Walk at a gradual grade along the steep wooded slope above Eagle Creek and after 0.7 mile traverse a sheer rock wall several hundred feet above the stream. Cables have been installed along the more exposed portions. Continue along a slightly less precipitous slope, traveling through woods and occasional small grassy patches. At 1.5 miles a side loop descends to the viewpoint of Metlako Falls. A short distance farther hop across Sorenson Creek on cement discs, traverse out of the little side canyon formed by the stream and come to a sign stating Lower Punchbowl Falls marking a side path that descends to the

shore of Eagle Creek. Keep left on the main trail and soon pass a fine viewpoint 100 feet above the Punchbowl.

Two hundred feet beyond the Punchbowl cross Tish Creek on a steel footbridge and later cross an unnamed stream on a similar span. At 3.0 miles hike above a narrow gorge of vertical rock walls and at the southern end cross the 80 foot deep chasm on High Bridge. After three-quarters mile recross Eagle Creek on another bridge and continue traversing through woods. Cross Wy'east Creek on a bridge of halved logs and just beyond it pass the first of many good campsites. A short distance farther cross a larger stream on a similar log bridge and near 5.3 miles pass the junction of the Eagle-Benson Way Trail that climbs steeply to Camp Smokey on the southern edge of the Benson Plateau. Keep right on the main trail and cross a large scree slope. At 6.0 miles traverse in and out of the side canyon that holds Tunnel Falls, pass another impressive waterfall then travel alongside Eagle Creek. Pass several good campsites downslope from the trail and cross two side streams before coming to the junction of the West Fork Eagle Creek Trail at 7.6 miles.

Turn sharply left and climb through woods. Recross the two streams you forded before the switchback and 200 yards beyond the second one pass a campsite on your right. At 9.3 miles come to Inspiration Point and a fine view of Lower Eagle Creek Gorge. Turn sharply right and traverse through deep woods for 0.5 mile to the junction of the Indian Springs Trail (see No. 21). Continue traversing uphill, passing campsites at 11.0 and 12.0 miles, and at 13.3 miles come to Wahtum Lake.

If you plan to return along Benson Plateau turn left onto No. 2000. To reach the most satisfactory campsites at the lake keep straight (right) and continue along the south shore.

Tunnel Falls

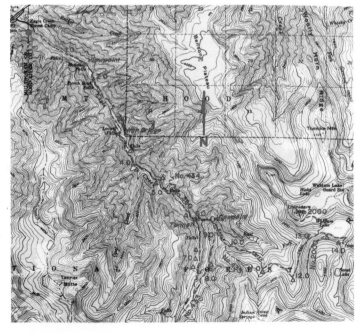

13 BENSON PLATEAU

Backpack
Distance: 14 miles one way
Elevation gain: 4,940 feet; loss 930 feet
High point: 4,200 feet
Allow 8 to 9 hours one way
Usually open June through November
Topographic map:
U.S.G.S. Bonneville Dam, Oreg.-Wash.
15'   1957

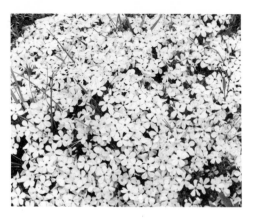

This hike follows the first 14 miles of the Pacific Crest National Scenic Trail in Oregon and the scenery along the route is appropriately impressive for the gateway to the state. After winding up to the rim of a 3,600-foot wall the trail traverses the length of the Benson Plateau near its eastern edge then generally follows a ridge crest, passing several good viewpoints, to Wahtum Lake.

You can do the backpack as a loop by returning along the Herman Creek Trail (No. 14) or, by establishing a short car shuttle, you could descend through Eagle Creek Gorge (No. 12). Also, since the trip ends at a road, it is possible to do the trek one way only. (See No. 20 for driving directions to the south end of the trail.) Carry adequate water as none may be available along the trail.

If you are approaching from the west drive on I 80N to the town of Cascade Locks. Go 0.9 mile through the business section to a sign pointing to Industrial Park and Airport. Keep left and after 1.9 miles cross the freeway on an overpass. Turn left and go 0.4 mile to a sign identifying the Columbia Gorge Work Center. Ample parking space is available in the vicinity of the Center. From the east drive 8.5 miles west of the Viento State Park interchange to the exit marked by a sign stating Herman Creek and Forest Lane. Turn left, go under the freeway then turn right and travel west along the frontage road for 0.7 mile to the sign identifying the Work Center. The trail begins at the west end of the Center beyond the large green equipment garage.

Climb in several short switchbacks for 0.3 mile to the power line road. Turn right and walk up its rocky bed for 130 yards to a sign marking the resumption of the Pacific Crest Trail and turn left. Wind up for 120 yards to the junction of the route to Herman Creek, Gorton Creek and Nick Eaton Ridge Trails (No's. 14, 15 and 16).

Keep straight (right), curve around the corner and climb in one set of switchbacks. Descend along an open slope then enter deep woods and begin walking along an old road. Pass a large camp and veer left onto the trail, as indicated by a sign and drop to the bridge across Herman Creek. Cross the span and traverse up then wind through a hummocked area of trees and rocks. Walk along the base of a large scree slope, switchback left and recross the rocks. (The trail heading west from the switchback eventually will be the new route of the Pacific Crest Trail that will begin at Cascade Locks.) Enter woods and make two sets of switchbacks then traverse and cross to the west side of the slope. Climb in irregular switchbacks for one mile then continue uphill along a ridge crest, coming to a helispot and good rest stop at 5.0 miles.

Continue climbing through open areas and woods to the northeastern edge of the Benson Plateau. Travel almost on the level along its eastern edge across sparsely wooded terrain, keeping left on the main trail at all paths leading off to the west. Near the southeast end of the plateau begin descending along the eastern slope, reenter woods and at 9.1 miles come to Camp Smokey. Hike near or along the ridge crest in stretches of level, downhill and uphill for 0.8 mile to a good viewpoint at a second helispot. Climb through a portion of the area that was burned in 1972 and descend along a wooded slope then walk along a crest to a saddle. Begin traversing along the open, southwestern slope of Chinidere Mountain (No. 20) then pass the junction of the spur to the summit. Keep straight on the main trail and after 60 yards come to a junction on your right. Veer right to reach Wahtum Lake and the Eagle Creek Trail or keep straight (left) to reach Road N20 and the Herman Creek Trail.

Bridge of the Gods

14 HERMAN CREEK TRAIL

Backpack
Distance: 12 miles one way
Elevation gain: 3,835 feet
High point: 3,950 feet
Allow 6 to 7 hours one way
Usually open June through November
Topographic map:
U.S.G.S. Bonneville Dam, Oreg.-Wash.
15'   1957

Originally, the northernmost section of the Pacific Crest (Skyline) Trail in Oregon was along Eagle Creek but because of the exposure the route was moved east to Herman Creek. However, portions of this second choice were, at that time, extremely swampy and the Trail was relocated again to its present route along the Benson Plateau. Most of the Herman Creek Trail traverses a densely wooded valley and for a change of scenery you could return along one of two different routes (see No. 13) or you can do the trip one way only (see No. 19).

From the west proceed on I 80N to the town of Cascade Locks. Go 0.9 mile east through the business section to a sign pointing to Industrial Park and Airport. Keep left and after 1.9 miles cross the freeway on an overpass. Turn left and go 0.4 mile to a sign identifying the Columbia Gorge Work Center. Ample parking space is available in the vicinity of the Center. From the east drive 8.5 miles west of the Viento State Park interchange to the exit marked by a sign stating Herman Creek and Forest Lane. Turn left, go under the freeway then turn right and travel west along the frontage road for 0.7 mile to the Work Center. The trail begins at the west end of the Center beyond the large, green equipment garage and is identified by signs.

Climb in several short switchbacks for 0.3 mile to a power line road. Turn right and walk for 130 yards to a sign stating Pacific Crest Trail and turn left. Wind up for 120 yards to the junction of the trail to the Benson Plateau (No. 13) and turn left. Climb steeply then more moderately for a few hundred yards to a flat, open area. Continue in the same direction you were heading and hike for 0.5 mile along the road that climbs gradually to the east high above Herman Creek to a camp on your left and the junction of the Gorton Creek Trail (No. 15).

Continue walking along the level road, soon passing the junction of the Nick Eaton Trail (No. 16) and continue to signs marking the beginning of the Herman Creek Trail. The road soon narrows and the route travels at a gradual downhill grade, passing the bases of two high waterfalls. Beyond the second, larger cascade begin climbing and at 2.6 miles travel in and out of the large side canyon formed by Camp Creek then descend slightly into a second, smaller ravine. At 3.9 miles keep straight (right) at the junction of Casey Creek Way that climbs to the crest of Nick Eaton Ridge and a few yards farther come to a clearing at 4 Mile Camp and the junction of the West Fork Trail. Keep straight (left) and cross the beds of two streams that may be dry then ford Slide, Mullinix and Whiskey Creeks. Travel through an area of several small streams before walking on the level to the junction of the Herman Creek Cutoff Trail to Rainy Lake. Keep straight (right) and almost immediately come to the Cedar Swamp Shelter. Water is available a short distance farther along the trail and this is a good choice for a lunch stop or a camp.

Continue along the main trail at an almost level grade and travel through a swampy area where the trail has been built higher than the surrounding terrain. Come to the East Fork of Herman Creek and a short distance beyond the crossing pass 7½ Mile Camp. Resume climbing along increasingly open slopes, switchback a few times and at 8.3 miles come to the junction of the short spur to Mud Lake. Keep right (straight) and traverse along an open area low on the southeastern shoulder of Tomlike Mountain. Continue climbing to the top of the ridge where a side path heads north to Tomlike Mountain (No. 19), curve left and follow the main route as it climbs along the crest. Enter deeper woods and travel at a gentle grade before the final, short climb to Road N20.

Along the Herman Creek trail

39

15 GORTON CREEK TRAIL

One day trip or backpack
Distance: 4 miles one way
Elevation gain: 2,395 feet; loss 250 feet
High point: 2,500 feet
Allow 3 hours one way
Usually open April through November
Topographic map:
U.S.G.S. Bonneville Dam, Oreg.-Wash.
15'   1957

Indian Point is an imposing 50-foot rock spire high on the steep face of the Columbia Gorge west of Wyeth. A side path near the end of the hike descends to this outcropping. The main trail continues another 0.5 mile to Deadwood Camp, a good site for an overnight stay. You can descend across large, open slopes on the return trip by following a portion of the Nick Eaton Ridge Trail (No. 16). This circuit would lessen the distance by a few tenths mile but add 330 feet of climbing.

From the west drive on I 80N to the town of Cascade Locks. Go 0.9 mile through the business section to a sign pointing to Industrial Park and Airport. Keep left and after 1.9 miles cross the freeway on an overpass. Turn left and go 0.4 mile to a sign identifying the Columbia Gorge Work Center. Ample parking space is available in the vicinity of the Center. From the east drive 8.5 miles west of the Viento State Park interchange to the exit marked by a sign stating Herman Creek and Forest Lane. Turn left, go under the freeway then turn right and travel west along the frontage road for 0.7 mile to the sign identifying the Work Center. The trail begins at the west end of the Center beyond the large equipment garage and is identified by signs.

Climb in several short switchbacks for 0.3 mile to a power line road. Turn right and walk up its rocky bed for 130 yards to a sign marking the resumption of the Pacific Crest Trail and turn left. Wind up for 120 yards to the junction of the trail to the Benson Plateau (No. 13) and turn left, following the sign pointing to Herman Creek Trail (No. 14). Climb steeply then more moderately for a few hundred yards to a flat, open area at 0.7 mile. Continue in the same direction you were heading and hike for 0.5 mile along the road that climbs gradually to the east high

above Herman Creek. Pass a "Water" sign on your right, marking a path that descends for 100 yards to a pipe and 150 feet farther along the road come to Herman Creek Camp in a flat, level clearing on your left. An outhouse is located beyond the northwest edge of the camp.

Turn left, walk several yards through the open area to a sign marking the beginning of the Gorton Creek Trail and follow an old roadbed up through woods for one-fifth mile. The road narrows into a trail that continues climbing. Traverse in and out of two small ravines then climb in two sets of switchbacks and traverse along the slopes of a large gully. Switchback twice, enter a second broad side valley and cross a small stream. Traverse over the crest of a ridge then several yards farther switchback right and travel in a southerly direction a short distance. Switchback at the crest of another ridge and come to the junction of the Ridge Cutoff Trail. On your way back turn here to make the recommended loop.

Keep straight (left) on the main trail and begin descending. Forty yards from the junction be watching for a pyramid shaped, decaying stump on the left side of the trail where a faint path heads downslope. To reach Indian Point wind steeply down this path for 0.2 mile to the open ridge at the base of the outcropping. The main trail generally continues downhill at a moderate grade. At 3.9 miles curve right and climb for a few yards to a sign marking the obscure junction of abandoned Deadwood Way. Turn left to a stream crossing. One hundred yards from the flow be looking downslope for a small open, flat area, the site of Deadwood Camp. The main trail soon turns south and after two miles reaches the crest of Nick Eaton Ridge.

Trail signs near Indian Point   *Indian Point*

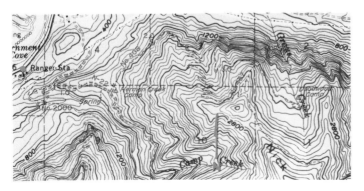

16 NICK EATON RIDGE

One day trip
Distance: 4.4 miles one way
Elevation gain: 3,965 feet; loss 200 feet
High point: 4,080 feet
Allow 3 to 3½ hours one way
Usually open late May through November
Topographic map:
  U.S.G.S. Bonneville Dam, Oreg.-Wash.
  15'   **1957**

The route to Nick Eaton Ridge crosses several large, open slopes that afford views of the Herman Creek drainage, the Benson Plateau and the Columbia River. This climb is a good choice for hikers who want a strenuous but relatively short trip. For even more exercise, the trail continues south for another three miles to Green Point Mountain. A short loop is possible by taking a connector at 3.1 miles to the Gorton Creek Trail (No. 15).

From the west proceed on I 80N to the town of Cascade Locks. Go 0.9 mile through the business district to a sign pointing to Industrial Park and Airport. Keep left and after 1.9 miles cross the freeway on an overpass. Turn left and go 0.4 mile to the Columbia Gorge Work Center, where you will find ample parking. From the east drive 8.5 miles west of the Viento State Park interchange to the exit marked by a sign stating Herman Creek and Forest Lane. Turn left, go under the freeway then turn right and travel west along the frontage road for 0.7 mile to the Work Center. The trail begins at the west end of the Center beyond the large green equipment garage and is identified by signs.

Climb in several short switchbacks for 0.3 mile to the power line road. Turn right and walk up its rocky bed for 130 yards to a sign marking the resumption of the Pacific Crest Trail and turn left. Wind up for 120 yards to the junction of the trail to the Benson Plateau (No. 13) and turn left, as indicated by the sign pointing to Herman Creek Trail (No. 14). Climb steeply then more moderately for a few hundred yards to a flat, open area at 0.7 mile. Continue in the same direction you were heading and hike for 0.5 mile along the road that climbs gradually to the east high above Herman Creek. Pass a sign stating "Water" on your right marking a path that

decends for 100 yards to a pipe, the last source of water along the hike, and 150 feet farther along the road come to Herman Creek Camp on your left and the junction of the Gorton Creek Trail. An outhouse is located beyond the northwest edge of the camp. Continue walking along the road at an almost level grade for 75 yards to a sign on your left marking the beginning of the Nick Eaton trail.

Turn left onto the trail and climb through woods, switchbacking periodically. Pass through a small, open area then travel in the woods before switchbacking up through a second, larger open slope. Reenter woods and come to a third, even more extensive clearing. Again reenter timber and climb along the crest of a ridge. Drop slightly then climb a short distance to the junction of the Ridge Cutoff Way to the Gorton Creek Trail. (This is the route of the optional return loop.)

Keep right on the main route and traverse up an open slope then reenter woods and after a short distance begin descending. Continue downhill to a saddle then climb along a wooded crest at a moderate grade to the junction of the abandoned Deadwood Trail. Keep straight (right) and begin climbing more steeply along the crest. The route curves left where the slope broadens and begins rising very steeply. The trail reaches the top of the ridge then traverses below it twice before traveling on the level through woods and climbing to the crest for a third time. Hike along the summit and a short distance after the trail begins losing elevation turn up to the left to a cluster of large boulders on the crest. This spot is a protected stopping place and from here you will be able to see the flat crest of the Benson Plateau, Mt. Defiance to the east and many other landmarks.

Near Nick Eaton trail

Bracket fungus

17 NORTH LAKE

One day trip or backpack
Distance: 5.5 miles one way
Elevation gain: 3,930 feet
High point: 4,070 feet
Allow 4 to 4½ hours one way
Usually open June through November
Topographic map:
    U.S.G.S. Bonneville Dam, Oreg.-Wash.
    15'   **1957**

Fishermen probably will want to try their luck at North Lake and any non-angling companions will be glad to lounge along the shore, resting from the strenuous climb. During the first part of the hike the route passes through several open areas that afford good views down onto the Columbia River and the Washington side of the Gorge in the vicinity of Wind Mountain and beyond to Mount Adams and St. Helens. Several sections of this trail are very steep so the trip is an excellent conditioning hike. The distance can be extended an additional 1.1 miles by continuing to Rainy Lake, situated on a bench below Green Point Mountain.

Drive on I 80N (the Columbia River Highway) ten miles east of the Bonneville Dam interchange or 13 miles west of Hood River to the Wyeth interchange. At the end of the exit turn south, as indicated by the sign point-int to Herman Creek Road, then turn left (east) and continue 0.2 mile, paralleling the eastbound entrance to the freeway, to a rock shop and a few other small buildings on your right. Park in the open area north of the road. The Wyeth Trail begins at the sign located between the cabins and the rock shop and house.

Follow a grassy, old road bed for several yards then climb through an open, brushy area. Pass under power lines at the southern, upper end of the clearing and enter woods. Soon begin curving east then switchback several times. Traverse across a small, open rocky slope where you can see west along the wall of the Gorge to Indian Point and to the north. Switchback left and cross the upper part of the scree slope and begin climbing steeply. At 1.6 miles abruptly curve left and begin traversing along the wall of the side canyon whose opposite slope forms the eastern side of Nick Eaton Ridge (No. 16). The trail makes one set of very short switchbacks and continues rising steeply. Hike at a moderate grade then drop slightly before climbing even more steeply to the stream crossing at 2.0 miles, a good place to take a rest before resuming the trek.

Cross the flow and climb very steeply in a few short switchbacks along the small canyon formed by the stream. Enter a grove of trees and wind up a narrow crest to a large open rocky area with a view of Carson and other landmarks to the north. Hike up through the open slope, reenter woods and begin climbing at a considerably more moderate grade. Curve east and soon begin a series of switchbacks. Near 3.8 miles come to the ridge crest and walk along it to the junction of the path to Nick Eaton Ridge. Keep left on the main trail and traverse at a very moderate grade along the east facing slope. About 0.5 mile from the junction come to a good viewpoint of Mt. Defiance (No. 18) east across the valley. In 1972 a microwave tower replaced the high, wooden lookout that formerly stood on the summit. Mt. Defiance is the highest point in the Columbia Gorge. Mt. Hood, the highest summit in Oregon, also can be seen from this viewpoint.

Descend moderately and cross a small stream then resume climbing. Hop over two more small flows that may dry up later in the summer and continue at an uneven grade. Walk along the edge of a small brushy area, watching for silver colored metal tags on trees where the trail is faint. Jump two more creeks and climb a short distance to a fork. Turn right and walk the final few yards to the north end of the lake at an old rock dam.

To reach Rainy Lake keep left at the fork and walk 75 yards to a junction where the right branch climbs to Rainy Lake and the trail to the left goes to Mt. Defiance.

Mt. Defiance

North Lake

18 MT. DEFIANCE

One day trip or backpack
Distance: 6 miles one way
Elevation gain: 4,815 feet
High point: 4,960 feet
Allow 4 to 5 hours one way
Usually open June through October
Topographic map:
   U.S.G.S. Hood River, Oreg.-Wash.
   15'   1957

Warren Lake

Mt. Defiance is the highest point in the Columbia Gorge and the view from its broad summit includes the fertile Upper and Lower Hood River Valleys, the Columbia River and Mounts St. Helens, Rainier, Adams and Hood. A short side trip involving an additional 1.5 miles and 560 feet of elevation loss and subsequent gain can be made to Warren Lake on the northeastern shoulder of Mt. Defiance. Since much of the trail rises at a moderately steep grade and the elevation gain is almost 5,000 feet, mountaineers frequently use this ascent as a conditioning climb.

Approaching from the west proceed on I 80N (the Columbia River Highway) to Starvation Creek State Park located 10 miles east of the Bonneville Dam interchange. (After the hike you will have to drive east along the freeway for one mile to the Viento State Park interchange.) From the east, drive 14 miles west of Hood River to the Wyeth interchange then head east on the freeway for 4.1 miles to Starvation Creek State Park. Ample parking is available here. A small sign at the west end of the exit lane identifies the Mt. Defiance Trail.

Walk parallel to the freeway along the south side of a wire fence for 100 yards then travel on the Old Columbia River Highway and pass Cabin Creek Falls. Hike through woods for a short distance before coming to a large clearing. Turn left (south), as indicated by a sign, and cross the grassy area below Hole-in-the-Wall Falls. Make an easy ford of Warren Creek and traverse west for a few hundred feet before coming to the junction of the Warren Falls Trail. Keep straight (right), soon pass just below Lancaster Falls and continue traversing along the slope where wild flowers are abundant during late May. Come to a sign at a faint junction and keep left on the main trail. Climb in a series of short switchbacks then enter a side can-

yon where a sign stating Water marks a short side path on your left to a spring, *the last source of water along the hike.*

Switchback up the wooded slope to a small viewpoint above Lindsey Creek canyon. Walk along a grassy, old road bed for several yards then climb along a shaded slope and switchback to a second small viewpoint. Continue uphill to a 0.3 mile long level stretch along a ridge crest and at the end of this respite resume climbing. Walk along another faint old road bed for several yards and soon begin climbing more steeply. Come to a viewpoint in an open area then resume climbing through woods. Begin curving left and hike at a more moderate grade along a ridge crest forested with small trees. Leave the timber and climb at a steeper grade to another fine viewpoint. Continue winding up the open slope before beginning an almost level traverse across rocky terrain and at 5.1 miles come to the junction of the faint Mitchell Point Trail down to Warren Lake, where you will find camping spots.

Keep right on the main route, climb moderately and enter deep woods just before coming to a well-defined road. Turn right, walk up the road for 40 feet to the resumption of the trail and wind up through woods. Where you rejoin the same road you can either turn left and follow it for the short distance to the summit or follow the path directly to the top. A rocky viewpoint on the east side of the wide summit affords good views of the Hood River area and the overlook on the western edge looks down onto Bear Lake.

To visit Warren Lake, descend along the rocky, faint path you passed at 5.1 miles. Stakes frequently mark the way. Two-tenths mile from the junction come to a viewpoint several hundred feet above the lake.

Mt. Adams from Mt. Defiance

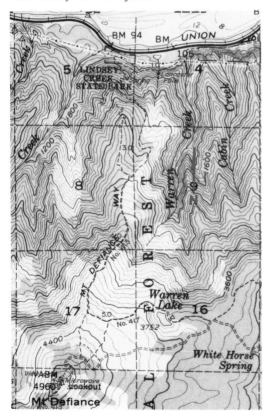

19 TOMLIKE MOUNTAIN

One-half day trip
Distance: 1.8 miles one way
Elevation gain: 400 feet; loss 200 feet
High point: 4,549 feet
Allow 1 hour one way
Usually open late June through October
Topographic map:
  U.S.G.S. Bonneville Dam, Oreg.-Wash.
  15'   1957

Tomlike Mountain is a massive ridge north of Wahtum Lake in the Columbia Gorge. Unlike most of the peaks in the Mt. Hood area the slopes of Tomlike Mountain have few tall trees. Fir groves slowly are establishing themselves along the burned slope but primarily the vegetation consists of grass and scattered clumps of dense, scrubby trees. During the climb of the long summit ridge you will have good views of the Herman Creek drainages and the eastern side of the Benson Plateau. Although the path is faint in some places, the route always is obvious. Since the hike is not long, you also could make the 0.7 mile, easy climb of Chinidere Mountain (No. 20) nearby to the southwest.

Drive on US 26 to the Lolo Pass Road at Zigzag, located 18 miles east of Sandy and two miles west of Rhododendron. Turn north and proceed 11.0 miles to Lolo Pass. Begin traveling downhill and continue on the Lolo Pass Road (N18) for 12.6 miles to the junction of N13. Turn left onto N13 and go 4.5 miles to the junction of N118. Turn right and continue on N118 — do not take any side spurs — for 5.8 miles to the junction with N20 above Wahtum Lake. (If you are approaching from the Hood River area go south from Hood River on Oregon 281 for 12 miles to the junction of the road to the plywood mill at the settlement of Dee. Veer right, leaving the highway, cross the Hood River then turn left and follow the signs pointing to Lost Lake for 5.0 miles to the junction of N13, 0.6 mile beyond the bridge across the West Fork of the Hood River. Keep right, travel on N13 for 4.5 miles to the junction of N118, turn right and follow N118 for 5.8 miles to N20.)

Turn right onto N20 and after 1.5 miles pass a turnout on your left and a sign marking the beginning of the hike to Chinidere Mountain. Early in the season or after heavy rains you probably will need to leave your car here as the road beyond can be very muddy. How-

ever, if the surface is dry curve right and continue on N20 three-quarters mile to a sign indicating the beginning of the Herman Creek Trail on your left just before the Wahtum Lake Warehouse. Ample parking space is available northeast of the building.

Descend for a short distance then walk at a gradual downhill grade along a gentle, wooded slope. Near 0.3 mile pass the junction of a proposed new section of the Herman Creek Trail on your left that meets N20 a short distance west of the trailhead at the warehouse. Begin descending on a ridge crest and where the main trail curves sharply right and traverses downhill keep straight (left) on the path marked by a sign reading Tomlike Mountain. The small body of water below to the east is Mud Lake and if you want to visit it, follow the main trail downhill for 0.7 mile to the short spur to the southwestern shore. Trail No. 406 continues and ends at the Columbia Gorge Work Center east of Cascade Locks. (For a detailed description of this route refer to No. 14.)

Hike along the crest through a forest of small evergreens and keep right where an abandoned unmarked path heads downhill to the West Fork of Herman Creek. As you gradually climb to the north the trees become sparse and the trail increasingly faint. Come to a saddle at 1.0 mile and continue on the broad crest. Near the summit of the first rise above the saddle keep right where you come to a patch of low, very dense trees sprawled over the crest. Beyond this slight detour the route continues up the open, rocky ridge top for 0.5 mile to the summit.

Tomlike Mountain from the south

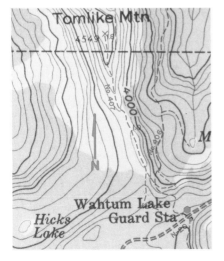

20 CHINIDERE MOUNTAIN

One-half day trip
Distance: 0.7 mile one way
Elevation gain: 425 feet
High point: 4,673 feet
Allow 30 minutes one way
Usually open late June through October
Topographic map:
    Bonneville Dam, Oreg.-Wash.
    15'   1957

Although not an especially high peak, Chinidere Mountain is so situated that the view from its rocky summit is exceptionally far-ranging: from Mounts St. Helens, Rainier and Adams and the Goat Rocks to the north you can look south to Mt. Hood, Ollalie Butte and Mt. Jefferson. Closer are the heavily wooded slopes of the Herman Creek drainage to the northeast, Tanner Butte and the Eagle Creek basin to the west and Wahtum Lake directly below to the southeast. Carry water as none is available along the trip.

Since the climb is so short and easy, you may want to extend the hike by continuing northwest along the main trail toward the Benson Plateau (see No. 13 for a description of this route). Also, you could combine the climb of Chinidere Mountain with the 1.8 mile long ascent of Tomlike Mountain (No. 19), nearby to the northeast.

Proceed on US 26 to the Lolo Pass Road at Zigzag, located 18 miles east of Sandy and two miles west of Rhododendron. Turn north and drive 11.0 miles to Lolo Pass. Begin traveling downhill and continue on the Lolo Pass Road (N18) for 12.6 miles to the junction of N13. Turn left onto N13 and go 4.5 miles to the junction of N118. Turn right and continue on N118 — 'do not take any side spurs — for 5.8 miles to the junction with N20 above Wahtum Lake. (If you are approaching from the Hood River area go south from Hood River on Oregon 281 for 12 miles to the junction of the road to the plywood mill at the settlement of Dee. Veer right, leaving the highway, cross the Hood River then turn left and follow the signs pointing to Lost Lake for 5.0 miles to the junction of N13, 0.6 mile beyond the bridge across the West Fork of the Hood River. Keep right, travel on N13 for 4.5 miles to the junction of N118, turn right and follow N118 for 5.8 miles to N20.) Turn right on N20 and drive 1.5 miles to a turnout on your left where the road curves right and a sign marks the beginning of Benson Way. Parking space is available here for several cars.

Walk west along an old road bed for 100 yards then begin traveling on a trail. Traverse at a very gradual grade along the gentle, wooded slope for 0.2 mile and climb slightly for a short distance before passing the junction of the Pacific Crest Trail No. 2000 that descends for 0.5 mile to Wahtum Lake. Keep right and 60 yards farther come to the unmarked junction of the spur to the summit of Chinidere Mountain.

Turn right and climb through woods in short, moderately graded switchbacks. Indian paintbrush, columbine, penstemon and other wild flowers bloom beside the trail in July. Where the path forks just below the shale surrounding the summit area, take the right branch for a more moderate climb and continue uphill along the rocky, open area to the summit, the site of a former lookout cabin. Chinidere Mountain was named for the last ruling chief of the Wasco Indians.

North face of Mt. Hood from Chinidere Mountain

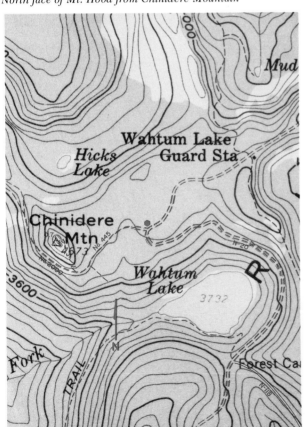

*Benchmark on summit,
Chinidere Mountain*

21 INDIAN MOUNTAIN

One day trip or backpack
Distance: 4.3 miles one way
Elevation gain: 1,400 feet; loss 200 feet
High point: 4,900 feet
Allow 2 hours one way
Usually open late June through October
Topographic map:
  U.S.G.S. Bonneville Dam, Oreg.-Wash.
  15'   1957

Excellent overviews of the upper Eagle Creek basin, one of the most remote areas in the Columbia Gorge, are enjoyed during portions of the final mile of the climb to Indian Mountain. The scene from the narrow, rocky summit includes Mt. Hood, Tanner Butte and many other landmarks in the Columbia Gorge. Water is available only at Indian Springs Camp at 3.1 miles.

A scenic, interesting loop with uncommon views can be made by taking Trail No. 435 that descends north from Indian Springs Camp to the Eagle Creek Trail (No. 12) and following the latter up to your starting point at Wahtum Lake. The loop would add 3.0 miles and 1,200 feet of climbing. If you want to shorten the climb to Indian Mountain by three miles you can drive along N20 to Indian Springs Camp.

Drive on US 26 to the Lolo Pass Road at Zigzag, located 18 miles east of Sandy and two miles west of Rhododendron. Turn north and proceed 11.0 miles to Lolo Pass. Begin traveling downhill and continue on the Lolo Pass Road (N18) for 12.6 miles to the junction of N13. Turn left onto N13 and go 4.5 miles to the junction of N118. Turn right and continue on N118 — do not take any side spurs — for 5.8 miles to the junction with N20 above Wahtum Lake. (If you are approaching from the Hood River area go south from Hood River on Oregon 281 for 12 miles to the junction of the road to the plywood mill at the settlement of Dee. Veer right, leaving the highway, cross the Hood River then turn left and follow the signs pointing to Lost Lake for 5.0 miles to the junction of N13, 0.6 mile beyond the bridge across the West Fork of the Hood River. Keep right, travel on N13 for 4.5 miles to the junction of N118, turn right and follow N118 for 5.8 miles to N20.) Ample parking

spaces are available off the road.

Switchback down to the southeast end of Wahtum Lake and follow the trail along the southern shore. Near the western end come to the junction of the Pacific Crest (Skyline) Trail No. 2000. Turn left and traverse up at a moderate grade along the wooded slope, periodically crossing a few small, open rocky areas. Descend slightly then climb to near N20. Walk parallel to and just below the road for a short distance then make a short set of switchbacks up a slope of large rocks where you can look south to Indian Mountain. Traverse through woods to a side road, cross to a sign listing several mileages and continue along the trail to Indian Springs Camp (picnic tables and outbuildings). Water can be obtained at the northwest edge of the area.

Follow the trail that climbs from the south side of the camp and head toward the open ridge above to the southwest then curve right and traverse up the slope to the crest. Trail No. 2000 crosses over the crest here and traverses south along the rocky western side of Indian Mountain. Turn left and climb moderately along the ridge top then cross N20 and follow an access road due south along the crest. Stay on the road where you pass an old metal sign at 4.2 miles and a short distance farther come to its end. Climb along a trail for 200 yards, switchbacking once, to the summit, the site of a former lookout cabin.

To make the loop descend steeply along No. 435 that begins across the stream at the northwest edge of Indian Springs Camp. Cross a scree slope where you can look east to Chinidere Mountain (No. 20) and the Benson Plateau (No. 13) and west to Tanner Butte (No. 8) then continue down to the Eagle Creek Trail. Turn right and climb 3.0 miles to Wahtum Lake.

Indian Mountain and ridge

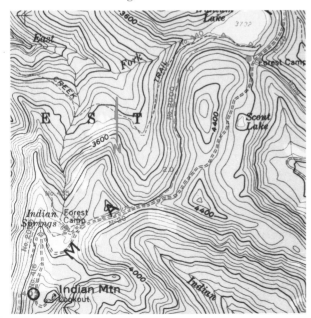

22 BALD BUTTE

One-half day trip
Distance: 1.5 miles one way
Elevation gain: 2,040 feet
High point: 3,779 feet
Allow 1 to 1½ hours one way
Usually open mid-March through November
Topographic map:
** U.S.G.S. Hood River, Oreg.**
** 15'   1957**

From the trailhead the grassy, treeless summit of Bald Butte seems deceptively close, but reaching it involves much steep climbing. Also, you probably will need to exercise some route finding ability on the return as the slopes on the middle portion of the hike are criss-crossed with a web of side paths. However, your efforts will be rewarded by an aerial-like view of the Upper Hood River Valley and a good vantage point for studying the northeast face of Mt. Hood. During late May and early June the big yellow blossoms of balsam root cover the open slopes below the summit and the flowering fruit trees on the valley floor form large patches of white. In the fall the yellows, rich browns and soft greens in the valley provide a different, but equally attractive, sight. Carry water as none is available along the route and include adequate clothing in your pack as the summit is almost always windy.

From I 80N drive 14.5 miles south of Hood River on Oregon 35 to the community of Mt. Hood. Continue on the highway 0.3 mile beyond the town to Hess Road and turn left (east). If you are approaching from the south proceed approximately 25.0 miles northeast on Oregon 35 from its junction with US 26 to Hess Road, located 0.7 mile beyond Tollbridge Park. Drive on the gravel road for 0.3 mile then curve left onto a dirt road, soon cross a canal and 0.7 mile from the highway come to a large bulldozed clearing. Be sure not to block the entrance to the excavation when you park your car. The road going east through woods from the northwest edge of the clearing is the beginning of the hike.

Climb moderately in woods along the road and walk above the upper, eastern end of the open swath. Continue up through woods and three-quarters mile from the trailhead come to a fork. The few aspen trees to the left are especially noticeable during the fall. Follow the left branch and after several yards come to a low bulldozed ridge. Drop from this rough area for a few yards and be watching for a path that heads up through slash from the left (north) side of the cat road. Climb steeply for 200 feet and meet a path traversing the grassy slope. Turn right and continue climbing. Turn around periodically and note the features of the terrain during this middle portion of the hike as the slopes are crisscrossed by a maze of side paths and you probably will not be returning along exactly the same route.

At 1.1 miles cross an old road bed and scramble up the opposite bank. Continue climbing moderately steeply, keeping right where you meet the many side paths, and begin curving right. Where you start traveling below the crest of a ridge the grade moderates and even drops slightly. The oaks and pines that covered the slopes midway along the climb gradually are replaced by Douglas fir as the elevation increases.

Come to the northwest edge of the open slope below the summit and note where the trail leaves the woods so you will be able to locate it easily on your return. Although the trail tread soon stops, the footing is satisfactory. Climb along the slope at about a 20° angle, aiming for the large, lone tree. When you reach it turn left and climb the final 150 yards to the summit of the long ridge. The lookout tower that once stood here was removed in 1973. If the west winds are strong you can usually find shelter on the east side of the ridge.

54

Hiker on crest of Bald Butte

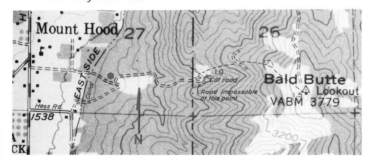

23 BUCK PEAK

One day trip
Distance: 7.5 miles one way
Elevation gain: 1,550 feet; loss 200 feet
High point: 4,751 feet
Allow 4 to 5 hours one way
Usually open late June through October
Topographic map:
U.S.G.S. Bull Run Lake, Oreg.
7.5'   1962

The route to Buck Peak traverses the ridge separating Bull Run and Lost Lakes, the two largest in the Mt. Hood area, and both are visible from viewpoints along the trail. The scene from the summit includes the rugged southern portion of the Columbia Gorge and the northwest face of Mt. Hood. Carry water as no good sources are available

With a car shuttle you can make a 25 mile backpack by continuing north from Buck Peak along the Pacific Crest Trail. From Indian Springs Camp (see No. 21) at 13.0 miles, the first satisfactory site for an overnight stay, you can complete the trek by following a spur to the Eagle Creek Trail (No. 12) or heading east a few miles to the Benson Plateau (No. 13) or Herman Creek (No. 14) Trails.

Proceed on US 26 to the Lolo Pass Road at Zigzag, located 18 miles east of Sandy and two miles west of Rhododendron, and turn north. Drive 11.0 miles to Lolo Pass where a sign on the left (north) side of the road identifies a section of the Pacific Crest Trail No. 2000 and lists several mileages. Parking spaces are available here and several yards farther off the east shoulder.

Walk on the level for a few hundred feet, climb through a cleared area under the transmission lines and begin traversing north at a steady, moderate grade. The northwest face of Mt. Hood looms across the valley to the east and farther on a sheer cliff face above the trail makes a photogenic frame for Mt. Adams. Near 0.9 mile cross a scree slope and resume traveling in woods. The grade becomes almost level along a bench then the trail drops slightly and winds across a saddle before traversing the east and north sides of Sentinel Peak. Cross a small open area and reenter attractive woods then drop slightly along a less vegetated slope. Reenter woods and at 4.0 miles follow an old firebreak for

0.1 mile to a saddle and the junction of the Huckleberry Mountain Trail that descends to Lost Lake (see No. 24).

Keep straight (left) on the Pacific Crest Trail, reenter woods and begin climbing. Pass a sign identifying Salvation Springs Camp, climb between Preachers Peak and Devils Pulpit in a few short switchbacks then resume traversing. Near 5.4 miles where the route travels several yards below a ridge crest be watching for a boulder slope above to your left. Scramble up over the rocks for a view down onto Bull Run Lake. Continue traversing along the wooded slope and soon have a good view down onto Lost Lake. Walk almost on the level along a broad ridge crest then resume traversing. At 6.3 miles where the trail curves sharply left along the face of the slope you will have the first view of your destination. Descend gradually for 0.5 mile then resume climbing moderately. Cross to the east side of the slope and 250 feet beyond the crest come to a sign marking the junction of the spur to the summit of Buck Peak. Keep right and wind up for one-quarter mile to the summit, the site of a former lookout cabin.

If you are making the backpack to the Columbia River, stay on the Pacific Crest Trail and soon begin switchbacking down. Traverse to the north for about 3.5 miles then walk below Road N20 for a short distance. Cross it and begin traversing the open west slope of Indian Mountain. One mile from N20 curve right, cross over the crest and descend for one-third mile to Indian Springs Camp.

Buck Peak from the east

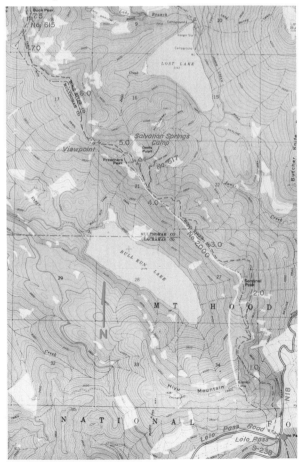

24 LOST LAKE TRAIL

One-half day trip
Distance: 3 miles round trip
Elevation gain: 100 feet
High point: 3,190 feet
Allow 1½ hours round trip
Usually open June through November
Topographic map:
  U.S.G.S. Bull Run Lake, Oreg.
  7.5'   1962

In August of 1880 a group of 12 men began a search for a large lake northwest of Mt. Hood that had been sighted earlier by two brothers. To commemorate their difficulty in finding the landmark, the men named it Lost Lake. Interestingly, another of the largest lakes in the Mt. Hood area, Bull Run Lake, is just to the south on the opposite side of a ridge. Since it is within the City of Portland's watershed, Bull Run Lake is closed to public access.

During the first portion of the level hike around Lost Lake, the firs and low bushes frame Mt. Hood perfectly and this section is popular with photographers. The remainder of the route continues along the wooded shore, often only inches from the water's edge. The trail may be swampy in a few places early in the season or after a period of rain.

You may want to combine this loop with the short climb of Lost Lake Butte (No. 25) that rises immediately to the east of the lake. The view from the summit is extensive and the two trips make a full day of hiking for those who prefer more exercise than just the trip around the shore.

Proceed on US 26 to the Lolo Pass Road at Zigzag, located 18 miles east of Sandy and two miles west of Rhododendron. Turn north and drive 11.0 miles to Lolo Pass. Begin driving downhill and continue on the Lolo Pass Road for 9.8 miles to Road S100 on your left identified by a sign stating Lost Lake 7. Stay on S100 to near the northeastern end of the lake then follow the signs pointing right to Store and Campground. From the small store and the cluster of buildings at the northern tip of the lake drive west, crossing the outlet creek, and continue 0.2 mile beyond the buildings to the large turnaround at the road's end where a sign stating Lake Shore Trail marks the beginning of the hike. If you are approaching from the Hood River area go south from Hood River on Oregon 281 for 12 miles to the junction of the road to the plywood mill at the settlement of Dee. Veer right, leaving the highway, cross the Hood River then turn left and follow the signs pointing to Lost Lake. Where you meet junctions that are both marked with signs stating Lost Lake take S100, the route with the lowest mileage, and continue to the trailhead as described above.

Walk on the level through attractive woods for three-quarters mile to a more open area at several inlet creeks. Boardwalks have been constructed along this stretch so crossing the delta presents no problems. Resume traveling through woods and near 0.9 mile, where the trail is about 200 feet from the lake, pass a dry campsite near the shore. This is a good place for a snack stop before finishing the hike.

Soon begin walking very near the shore and traverse a small scree slope before continuing beside the water's edge. Gain and lose some minor amounts of elevation then at the south end of the lake come to the junction of the Huckleberry Mountain Trail that climbs for 2.5 miles to the Pacific Crest Trail and the route to Buck Peak (No. 23). Keep left and farther on pass below some rustic buildings then continue along the trail for 0.7 mile to where it meets a road. Continue north on the road closest to the shore for 0.5 mile to reach your starting point.

Lost Lake and Mt. Hood

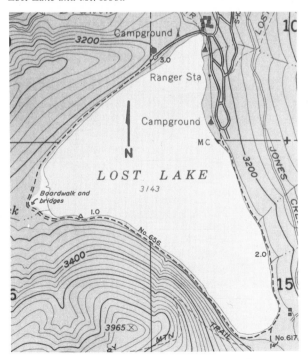

25   LOST LAKE BUTTE

One-half day trip
Distance: 2 miles one way
Elevation gain: 1,270 feet
High point: 4,468 feet
Allow 1 to 1½ hours one way
Usually open June through October
Topographic map:
   U.S.G.S. Bull Run Lake, Oreg.
   7.5'   1962

The western slope of Lost Lake Butte begins at the shore of Lost Lake and making both the climb to the summit of the peak and the level circuit around the wooded shore of the lake makes a pleasing combination of scenery. (See No. 24 for a description of the route around Lost Lake.) In addition to the major peaks — Mounts Hood, Jefferson, St. Helens and Adams — the summit of Lost Lake Butte also affords views of Hickman Butte, Mt. Defiance, Larch and Indian Mountains and the Upper Hood River Valley. Carry water as none is available along the trail.

Drive on US 26 to the Lolo Pass Road at Zigzag, located 18 miles east of Sandy and two miles west of Rhododendron. Turn north and proceed 11.0 miles to Lolo Pass. Begin driving downhill and continue on the Lolo Pass Road for 9.8 miles to Road S100 on your left identified by a sign stating Lost Lake 7. Follow S100 to near the northeast end of Lost Lake. Keep left at roads going west to the campground and the lake shore and continue on S102 to a sign on the right (west) shoulder pointing across the road to the beginning of the Lost Lake Butte Trail. Ample parking spaces are available along the sides of the road. If you are approaching from the Hood River area go south from Hood River on Oregon 281 for 12 miles to the junction of the road to the plywood mill at the settlement of Dee. Veer right, leaving the highway, cross the Hood River then turn left and follow the signs pointing to Lost Lake. Where you meet junctions that are both marked with signs stating Lost Lake follow S100, the route with the lowest mileage, to its junction with S102 and continue along the latter road to the sign marking the beginning of the Lost Lake Butte Trail.

The trail begins on the east side of the road and follows a gradual grade through deep woods for a short distance before climbing moderately along the slope. Near 0.8 mile rhododendron bushes become plentiful and as the trail gains elevation the trees become smaller and the vegetation less dense. During the final three-quarters mile to the summit the route makes several switchbacks of uneven length. Before reaching the top, the site of a former lookout cabin, you will have views of Lost Lake and Mounts Hood, St. Helens and Adams.

Aerial view of Lost Lake Butte

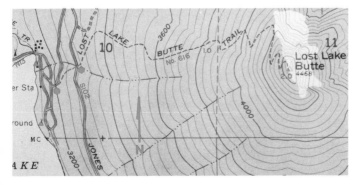

26   HIYU MOUNTAIN

One-half day trip
Distance: 1.4 miles one way
Elevation gain: 1,255 feet
High point: 4,654 feet
Allow 1 hour one way
Usually open late June through October
Topographic map:
   U.S.G.S. Bull Run Lake, Oreg.
   7.5'   1962

For many years the trail up Hiyu Mountain was closed to public travel but the route was reopened in 1973 and hikers again can make the easy ascent to the fine viewpoint on the summit. In addition to the proximity of the west face of Mt. Hood, flanked by Barrett Spur on the north, you will be able to identify Mounts St. Helens, Rainier and Adams along the northern horizon. The scene also includes landmarks in the Columbia Gorge and terrain south to Mt. Jefferson. Although the trail climbs for the entire distance, the grade is never severe. Carry water as none is available along the route.

Proceed on US 26 to the Lolo Pass Road at the community of Zigzag, located 18 miles east of Sandy and two miles west of Rhododendron. Turn north and drive 11.0· miles to the summit of Lolo Pass where a sign on the north (left) side of the road identifies a section of the Pacific Crest Trail No. 2000. Parking spaces are available here and at a small turnout several yards farther off the east shoulder of Lolo Pass Road.

Walk on the level for a few hundred feet through a cut then go under the Bonneville Power Administration transmission lines. Just beyond the lines turn left onto an old cat road and walk along it for 40 feet then scramble several yards up the bank on your right. Climb along the logged slope, veering slight-

ly right, for about 100 feet and if you already have not met an old cat road, curve right and continue several yards until you do. Climb on the cat road for 100 yards, switchback left and after several yards turn right onto a path at the edge of the timber. From here to the summit the route is a well-defined trail. Switchback left after 200 feet then traverse up along the face of the slope for a short distance. Curve right and climb to the north then begin traversing along a ridge. Some blowdown may block the trail but because of the nature of the terrain and vegetation, obstacles can be circumvented.

Continue climbing at a moderately steep grade, switchbacking at irregular intervals. At 1.2 miles travel along the crest of a narrow, short ridge. At its end traverse below the steep, open summit area of Hiyu Mountain. Where the trail becomes faint turn right and climb several feet to Road S130 that is closed to public travel. Walk northeast a few yards to the end of the road and turn right onto the path that climbs along the crest of the summit ridge. Just after leaving the road you can turn around and look northwest past an old fire break over Bull Run Lake. Continue along the crest for a few hundred feet, passing the site of the former fire lookout, to the end of the path at a little wooden bench.

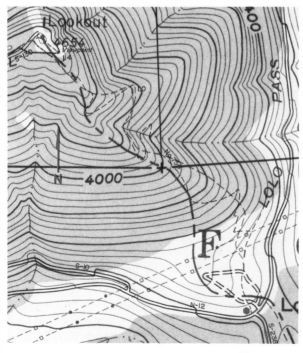

63

One day trip
Distance: 3.3 miles one way
Elevation gain: 1,310 feet; loss 140 feet
High point: 4,591 feet
Allow 2 hours one way
Usually open July through October
Topographic map:
  U.S.G.S. Bull Run Lake, Oreg.
  7.5'   1962

This short hike follows the Pacific Crest Trail south from Lolo Pass for 3.0 miles then climbs along a short spur path to the top of Bald Mountain, situated only three linear miles from the west face of Mt. Hood. The low bushes and scattered trees on the summit belie the name of the former lookout site but do not interfere with the fine, close-up view that includes such easily identified features as Illumination Rock, Reid and Sandy Glaciers and the spires on upper Yocum Ridge.

You can shorten the climb to Bald Mountain to two miles round trip by driving south from Lolo Pass on S238 for 3.1 miles then turning very sharply left onto S238J and continuing 1.3 miles to a sign on your right marking the Top Spur Trail No. 785. Hike up the trail for 0.5 mile to No. 2000, turn right and continue as described below.

Drive on US 26 to the Lolo Pass Road at Zigzag, located 18 miles east of Sandy and two miles west of Rhododendron, and turn north. Proceed 11.0 miles to Lolo Pass where a sign on the east (right) side of the road identifies the beginning of a section of the Pacific Crest Trail No. 2000 and lists mileages to the Timberline Trail and other destinations. Parking spaces are available here and along the north shoulder.

Walk south through a clearcut then enter woods and climb at a gradual grade. Make a series of short switchbacks above a stream then near 0.8 mile begin traversing. After one-third mile switchback and walk along the north facing slope of a small basin. Traverse above a pond and continue along the wall of the bowl. At 1.5 miles switchback left and begin traveling to the southeast, the direction you will be heading for the remainder of the hike. Climb to the rim of the basin where the trail levels off for a short distance. Resume traversing and hike along the south side of the ridge before rejoining the crest at

2.2 miles. Drop slightly then climb at a gradual grade. During one section the woods are replaced by more open terrain.

At 2.9 miles come to the junction of the Top Spur Trail and keep straight (left). One hundred fifty feet from the sign come to the junction of the Timberline Trail. The Bald Mountain shelter, one of the two wooden structures constructed when the Timberline Trail was built, stood on the level area just northwest of the junction. It had been unusable for several years and the remains were removed in 1973.

Continue south along No. 2000, the middle of the three trails, as indicated by the sign pointing to Bald Mountain. One hundred yards from the junction be watching for a trail, No. 600D on your left heading upslope. Follow this path, traveling parallel to the main route, then curve left. Climb more steeply for 0.1 mile then walk at a gradual grade just before reaching the summit. In addition to the close-up view of the west face of Mt. Hood you can look down into the rugged canyon at the head of the Sandy River and onto a portion of the Pacific Crest Trail. The three main ridges radiating from the west face are, from east to west, Barrett Spur, Cathedral Ridge and Yocum Ridge and trails (No's. 29, 28 and 51) visit each one.

Mt. Hood from the summit of Bald Mountain

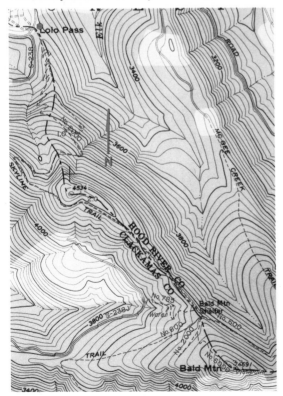

28 CATHEDRAL RIDGE

One day trip
Distance: 3 miles one way
Elevation gain: 2,210 feet
High point: 5,600 feet
Allow 2 hours one way
Usually open July through October
Topographic maps:
    U.S.G.S. Bull Run Lake, Oreg.
    7.5'   **1962**
    U.S.G.S. Cathedral Ridge, Oreg.
    7.5'   **1962**

The three mile long trail up the wooded, lower portion of Cathedral Ridge meets the Timberline Trail near a grassy swale just above some tarns, a lovely spot for a leisurely lunch. Mt. Hood fills the view above to the east and if you find this alpine setting more invigorating than relaxing you can follow the Timberline Trail east to Cairn Basin then make a loop through Wy'east Basin and Eden Park. This circuit would add four miles and 600 feet of elevation gain. A shorter, but also exceptionally scenic, trip is possible by continuing up the swale at the end of the Cathedral Ridge Trail to an old, but well worn, path then traversing south to the stone shelter on McNeil Point. (For detailed descriptions of these side trips refer to the appropriate sections of the Timberline Trail No. 59.) No water is available until the 3.0 mile point.

Proceed on US 26 to the Lolo Pass Road at Zigzag, located 18 miles east of Sandy and two miles west of Rhododendron, and turn north. Drive 11.0 miles to Lolo Pass then go downhill on the Lolo Pass Road for 3.3 miles to the junction of Road S19. Turn right and after 1.7 miles curve up to the left, following signs indicating the route to the Timberline and Cathedral Ridge Trails. Continue the final 2.7 miles to a clearcut where a sign on your left points to the trail. Parking spaces are available along the edges of the clearing.

During the spring of 1973 strong winds caused a tangle of blowdown on the ridge above the clearcut. Consequently, the trailhead may be located a few hundred yards farther along S19A than shown on the map. Regardless of the starting point, the route climbs for several hundred feet to the crest of the ridge above the clearcut then continues uphill. After a brief level stretch the trail begins rising even more steeply in a series of short switchbacks for 0.3 miles. Continue up along the wooded ridge at an erratic, but less severe, grade, at one point coming close to the rim of the steep slope above Ladd Creek canyon.

Near 1.7 miles walk through the length of a narrow, grassy clearing. At its southern end reenter woods and follow a faint trail for a short distance before beginning a mile long traverse of the ridge's steep western side. Pass through a swath of boulders near timberline then climb along the wall of the little valley that holds the tarns. A good lunch stop is beside a stream a few hundred yards up the swale from the tarns.

To make the side trip to Cairn Basin continue up the swale until you intersect the Timberline Trail and follow it to the northeast (left).

Beargrass

At rest along the trail

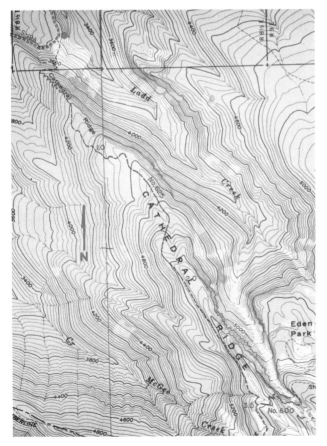

29 VISTA RIDGE and BARRETT SPUR

One day trip or backpack
Distance: 4.3 miles one way
Elevation gain: 3,355 feet
High point: 7,850 feet
Allow 3 to 3½ hours one way
Usually open late July through mid-October
Topographic map:
    U.S.G.S. Cathedral Ridge, Oreg.
    7.5'   **1962**

Barrett Spur is an immense rocky ridge 2,300 feet above Elk Cove and separates Ladd and Coe Glaciers on the north side of Mt. Hood. From the crest of the Spur you will be able to look across and down to the jumble of crevasses and seracs of these ice fields. If you do not care to make the 1.4 mile, cross-country ascent of the Spur, you can extend the hike by following an exceptionally scenic loop through Cairn Basin and Eden Park to the west or heading east to Elk Cove. (See the appropriate sections of the text for the Timberline trail, No. 59.)

Drive on US 26 to the Lolo Pass Road at Zigzag, 18 miles east of Sandy and two miles west of Rhododendron, and turn north. Proceed 11.0 miles to Lolo Pass then go downhill, continuing on N18 (the Lolo Pass Road), for 6.4 miles to the junction of S160. Turn right as indicated by the sign pointing to Vista Ridge Trail and after 0.9 mile turn left, staying on S160. Follow the road as it switchbacks right after 1.3 miles then keep left on S160 2.6 miles farther. Six-tenths mile beyond the last junction turn right onto N100, again following a sign to Vista Ridge Trail. Drive 2.8 miles from the junction to an unsigned fork, keep left (slightly uphill) and proceed the final 0.8 mile to the end of the passable road where a sign marks the beginning of the Vista Ridge Trail. Ample parking spaces are available. If you are approaching from the Hood River area proceed south on Oregon 281 or 35 to the west end of Parkdale and go west on Baseline Road for 1.0 mile to a junction and keep left, following the sign to Red Hill. Two-tenths mile farther keep straight (right) at the junction of N19 then a short distance farther keep left on N100. Stay on N100 for 17.0 miles, keep left at an unsigned fork and continue the final 0.8 mile.

The old road narrows to a path after 100 yards and enters woods. Hike on the level for 0.5 mile and come to the junction of the abandoned trail to Red Hill Guard Station. Bear right and traverse, then curve left into a small ravine. Make a set of short switchbacks and continue winding up through woods at a moderate grade. A few hundred yards beyond the first view of Mt. Hood come to the junction of the former route of the Timberline Trail that you will follow if you intend to make the loop. This circuit is 2.0 miles long and involves 300 feet of elevation gain. To continue the hike to Barrett Spur stay left on the old Timberline Trail and after traversing 0.2 mile come to Wy'east Basin and the junction of the new section of the Timberline Trail. To visit Elk Cove, two miles distant, keep left around "99" Ridge.

To reach the summit of Barrett Spur leave the established trail and climb to the southeast. Although finding the route up presents no problems, you should turn around frequently and familiarize yourself with features of the terrain so on the return you will have an equally easy job of locating where you left the Timberline Trail. After about 0.5 mile of cross-country reach the crest of the lower portion of the Spur. Climb along the ridge top and after another 0.5 mile come to a broad saddle below the rocky summit block. Although the grade increases considerably beyond here, the footing is good and you can climb at any comfortable angle. Come to the crest of the Spur and continue to another high point then descend slightly, being careful not to go near the edge of any of the steep snow slopes. Resume climbing and scramble over boulders for 0.1 mile to a broad, level area on the crest that is a good stopping place.

Coe Glacier from Barrett Spur

69

30 ELK COVE TRAIL

One day trip or backpack
Distance: 3.3 miles one way
Elevation gain: 1,500 feet
High point: 5,450 feet
Allow 2 hours one way
Usually open July through October
Topographic map:
   U.S.G.S. Cathedral Ridge, Oreg.
   7.5'   1962

Elk Cove is the most northerly and rugged of the several exceptionally scenic basins situated at timberline on the northern and northwestern slopes of Mt. Hood. Since the Timberline Trail (No. 59) passes through the Cove, you can extend the hike by following it east toward Cloud Cap or west toward Eden Park and Wy'east and Cairn Basins. A more strenuous side trip would be the climb of Barrett Spur (No. 29), the rocky ridge to the south that separates Coe and Ladd Glaciers. Because of the setting and the many possible side trips, Elk Cove is an excellent choice for a backpack or a one day hike.

Proceed on Oregon 35 to the road to Tilly Jane Campground and Cooper Spur located 15.7 miles northeast of the junction of Oregon 35 and US 26 and 24.3 miles south of Hood River. Turn west and after 2.4 miles keep straight (right). Five miles farther turn left, following the sign pointing to Laurence Lake and after 0.5 mile again turn left as indicated by the sign pointing to Laurence Lake. Two and one-half miles farther keep right then continue 1.2 miles to a junction just before the dam at Laurence Lake and keep straight. Six-tenths mile farther, beyond the lake, turn left at a sign pointing to Trail No. 630. Keep left after one mile, following the sign indicating the direction to Trail No. 631, and drive the final 1.3 miles to a sign that marks the beginning of the Elk Cove Trail. Limited parking space is available along the side of the road. If you are approaching from the Hood River area proceed south on Oregon 281 or 35 to the west end of the town of Parkdale then head south for three miles to a sign pointing right (west) to Laurence Lake. Turn right, continue 3.7 miles to near the end of Laurence Lake and continue to the trailhead as described above.

Traverse up the bank for several yards then curve right and continue uphill along the wooded slope. Make two very short switchbacks and hike on the ridge crest at a moderate grade. Periodically, you will have views of Mt. Hood. Travel above a logged area and reenter woods at the junction of the old Elk Cove Trail. Keep right on the main route and climb at a slightly steeper grade along the crest. Come to a good view of Mt. Hood and descend through a more open area. Pass the sign marking the Wilderness boundary then regain the elevation just lost and reenter woods. Where you pass a low rocky crest to your left a few feet above the trail, leave the main route and climb to the overlook for a view into Coe Creek gorge. Descend for a short distance along the main trail then resume climbing. The grade briefly is considerably steeper then it resumes the usual moderate angle. As the elevation increases the woods gradually become composed of large conifers. Walk almost on the level past dense patches of avalanche lilies that are prettiest in mid-July.

Make an easy ford of a wide, shallow stream and continue up through attractive woods past more clusters of the white lilies. The trail climbs up a ravine in several short, loose switchbacks then becomes straight for 0.1 mile and meets the Timberline Trail at the edge of Elk Cove. Turn right and walk 100 yards to the center of the basin. The remains of the stone shelter and the weathered tree trunks offer silent evidence of the avalanches that rush down the steep slopes enclosing the Cove.

Mt. Hood from Upper Hood River Valley

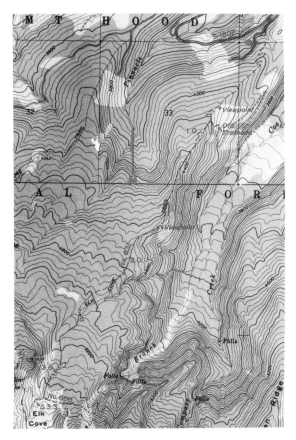

31 ZIGZAG TRAIL

One-half day trip
Distance: 1 mile one way
Elevation gain: 860 feet
High point: 3,720 feet
Allow 45 minutes to 1 hour one way
Usually open mid-April through November
Topographic map:
    U.S.G.S. Dog River, Oreg.
    7.5'   **1962**

This short hike begins at Pollalie Camp-ground and winds up through woods to a semi-open area where scattered pines frame a view of the east face of Mt. Hood and portions of the Upper Hood River Valley. The main trail continues another one-half mile to Road S16 near Clinger Spring.

Drive on Oregon 35 to Polallie Camp-ground located 15.7 miles northeast of the junction of US 26 and Oregon 35 and 24.3 miles south of Hood River. Turn east, enter the campground and leave your car at one of the parking areas.

Walk to the southwest end of the campground and cross a side stream on a pole bridge to a sign stating Zigzag Trail. Cross the East Fork of Hood River on a footbridge, climb several feet and switchback up to the left. The trail winds up at a moderately steep grade and crosses a small stream that flows down a heavily wooded little side canyon. This is the only source of water along the hike. Continue climbing in short switch-backs and at 0.4 mile traverse through deep woods in an easterly direction. Occasionally during portions of the trip you will have glimpses of Mt. Hood between the trees. The trail resumes climbing in short switchbacks and winds up between two large rock slides. At the crest of the ridge come to a sign point-ing right to Viewpoint 500 Feet. Descend along the spur and switchback once before coming to the end of the path in a clearing.

Trail bridge, East Fork Hood River

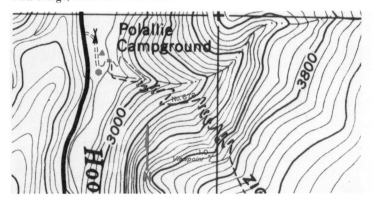

32 TILLY JANE SKI TRAIL

One day trip
Distance: 3.2 miles one way
Elevation gain: 2,050 feet
High point: 5,940 feet
Allow 2½ hours one way
Usually open mid-June through October
Topographic maps:
    U.S.G.S. Cathedral Ridge, Oreg.
    7.5'   **1962**
    U.S.G.S. Dog River, Oreg.
    7.5'   **1962**

Whereas the hike along the Alpine Ski Trail (No. 58) follows a run popular with downhill skiers, the path up Tilly Jane Ski Trail is along a route used mostly by cross-country skiers. The path climbs through woods and along small, grassy slopes to Tilly Jane Campground and a trail continues two-thirds mile farther to charming Cloud Cap Inn. You can make a short, very scenic loop at the end of the hike by climbing along Trail No. 600A from Tilly Jane Campground to the junction with the Timberline Trail just below Cooper Spur Shelter then following the route north down to Cloud Cap Inn. This highly recommended circuit would add two miles and 900 feet of elevation gain (see No. 34). Since roads go both to Tilly Jane Campground and Cloud Cap, it is possible to do the hike one way only. Be sure to start the hike with a full bottle as water may not be available until the campground.

Drive on Oregon 35 to the road to Tilly Jane Campground and Cooper Spur situated 15.7 miles northeast of the junction of US 26 and Oregon 35 and 24.3 miles south of Hood River. Turn west and after 2.4 miles turn left, following the sign to Cloud Cap and Tilly Jane. One mile farther keep left on the one-way road that goes to the Cooper Spur Ski Area and continue the final 0.7 mile to the large parking area near the edge of the ski slope. At the end of the hike drive along the spur loop for a short distance to rejoin Road S12.

Walk up the ski slope near the poma lift that runs along the western edge of the clearing to a road where a sign reads Tilly Jane Ski Trail and turn right. Enter woods and walk along the road. Curve left then where the road curves left again keep straight ahead on a path. A sign several yards farther identifies the route of the Tilly Jane Ski Trail. Walk at a gradual grade, drop slightly then begin climbing steeply. The grade eventually moderates then resumes rising steeply until it reaches a semi-open, broad ridge crest at 1.5 miles and curves right. Climb moderately along the crest, traverse for a short distance and return to the crest. Begin a longer traverse along the steep, northern slope then continue uphill through woods. Pass a large shelter at 2.7 miles and a short distance farther pass a second considerably smaller one at the southern edge of Tilly Jane Campground.

If you want to go directly to Cloud Cap continue straight ahead along the trail and after a few yards drop to Tilly Jane Creek. Climb and continue along the path at a gradual grade for 0.5 mile to a camping area at the junction of the Timberline Trail. Turn right and walk about 75 feet to the Cloud Cap Road (S12) then keep right and walk along it for several hundred yards to its end at a large turnaround. The building directly to the north is the Snow Shoe Club Lodge and Cloud Cap Inn is on the crest of the ridge to the south.

To make the recommended loop, head south on Trail 600A that begins a few yards to the west of the second, smaller shelter cabin at Tilly Jane Campground. Climb moderately through woods to the rim of Polallie Creek Canyon then continue up through the increasingly sparse and stunted timber to the Timberline Trail. Turn right and traverse along the rocky terrain to the junction with the northern segment of 600A at the Cloud Cap Road.

Mt. Hood from Tilly Jane campground

33 TAMANAWAUS FALLS

One-half day trip
Distance: 1.6 miles one way
Elevation gain: 440 feet
High point: 3,490 feet
Allow 1 hour one way
Usually open late April through November
Topographic map:
  U.S.G.S. Dog River, Oreg.
  7.5'   1962

Near Cold Spring Creek

The trail to Tamanawaus Falls traverses a narrow, wooded canyon beside rambunctious Cold Spring Creek before reaching the viewpoint near the base of the 100 foot high cascade. The hike is a good choice for a short, leisurely trip and several spots along the creek afford attractive places for snack stops. If you want to extend the hike you can continue along the main trail that eventually ends at Elk Meadows (see No. 35).

Drive on Oregon 35 for 14.5 miles east and north of the junction of US 26 and Oregon 35 or 25.5 miles south of Hood River to a large parking area off the west side of the highway where a sign states East Fork Trail No. 650. This turnout is one-quarter mile north of Sherwood Campground and one mile south of Polallie Campground.

The trail begins from the northwest edge of the turnout at a sign and winds through woods for a few hundred feet to a narrow footbridge across the East Fork of the Hood River. Hike parallel to the river and the highway for 0.4 mile, periodically traveling at a gradual uphill grade, to the edge of the canyon formed by Cold Spring Creek. Here you can look across the highway to an impressive formation of columnar basalt.

Turn sharply west and traverse for 150 yards to the junction of the trail from Polallie Campground. Keep left (straight), descend slightly and cross Cold Spring Creek on a footbridge. Climb moderately along the north bank of the creek, periodically passing through some brief swampy areas. The deep woods become somewhat more open as you hike up the canyon and the stream constantly is changing character.

Near the edge of a boulder field at 1.4 miles switchback right and after a short distance come to the junction of the trail to Elk Meadows. Turn left and traverse through woods to the upper portion of the boulder field. Cross the rocks below a high cliff band then reenter woods and continue along the slope for the final few hundred yards to the view of Tamanawaus Falls.

Tamanawaus Falls

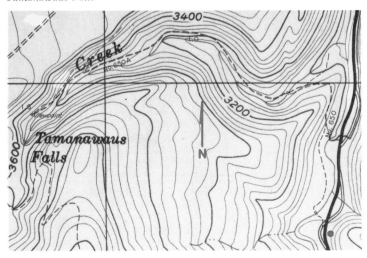

34 COOPER SPUR

One day trip
Distance: 3.5 miles one way
Elevation gain: 2,655 feet
High point: 8,514 feet
Allow 2½ to 3 hours one way
Usually open mid-July through early October
Topographic map:
   U.S.G.S. Cathedral Ridge, Oreg.
   7.5'   1962

Cooper Spur is the high, rocky ridge that separates Eliot and Newton Clark Glaciers on the northeast slopes of Mt. Hood. Eliot Glacier, the most extensive on the peak, also has the largest crevasses and the jumble of these yawning chasms is intriguing to observe. Even without the bird's-eye view of Eliot Glacier, this hike to the highest point visited in the guide would be an exceptionally scenic trek. From near Cloud Cap Inn the route follows the Timberline Trail then winds up the barren, rocky spur toward the steep, fearsome north face of Mt. Hood. Start the hike with a full bottle of water as the sources along the route are not dependable.

Drive on Oregon 35 to the road to Tilly Jane Campground and Cooper Spur situated 15.7 miles northeast of the junction of US 26 and Oregon 35 and 24.3 miles south of Hood River. Turn west and after 2.4 miles turn left, following the sign to Cloud Cap and Tilly Jane. Continue along S12, that eventually has a dirt surface, for 10 miles to the junction with the spur to Tilly Jane Campground. Keep right and drive the final three-quarters mile to a sign pointing right to the Timberline Trail. If the few parking spaces on the shoulder of the road are taken, continue up the road for several hundred yards to its end at a large turnaround just below Cloud Cap Inn.

Walk a few hundred feet into the woods as indicated by the sign and come to a three-way junction. Turn left onto the upper trail, not the lower one — 600A — to Tilly Jane Campground. Traverse through woods and after a couple hundred yards keep left on the main route at the junction of the side trail to Eliot Glacier. (You can reach Cooper Spur by taking this side path but a portion of the route is up an unstable scree slope that offers poor footing.) Continue up through woods of widely-spaced, thick-trunked conifers. Come to a moraine at timberline and climb along the slopes of sand and boulders, making a few short semi-switchbacks. Traverse the wall of a small rocky canyon then curve left and climb through a swath of stunted evergreens. Leave the vegetation and resume traversing a slope of rocks and scattered clumps of grass and other low growing plants. At 1.1 miles come to the junction of the trail from Tilly Jane Campground (see No. 32).

Turn right, leaving the Timberline Trail, and begin meandering up over the rocky terrain. After a few hundred feet pass the remains of the Cooper Spur Shelter off the trail to your right (north). The tread becomes more obvious as you gain elevation and the route travels parallel to and above the Timberline Trail for one mile beyond the junction. At 2.2 miles begin the first of several long switchbacks. The trail engineers took the altitude into consideration and designed a steady, moderate grade. During the climb views of Mounts Adams, St. Helens and Rainier and the Upper and Lower Hood River Valleys can be seen to the north and as you gain more elevation you will see Newton Clark Glacier to the southwest as well as Eliot Glacier below and across to the northwest. The switchbacks become considerably shorter before you reach a good stopping place at 3.5 miles just before the crest makes a dip. Elk Meadows, the largest on the slopes of Mt. Hood, below timberline on the southeast side of the mountain and Cloud Cap Inn on the top of the short ridge near the beginning of the hike are two of the many landmarks you can identify from this lofty perch. You can continue along the ridge, passing Tie-In Rock, for another one-quarter mile before reaching terrain that is unsuitable for hiking.

Idiographic inscription from Japanese climbing expedition of 1910

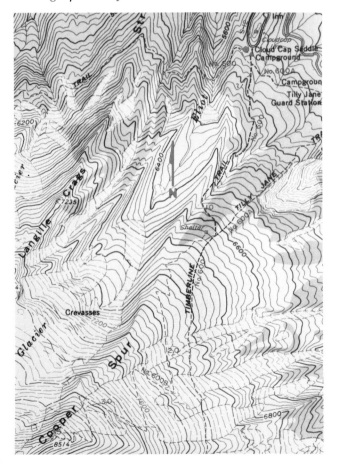

35 COLD SPRING CREEK TRAIL

One day trip or backpack
Distance: 7 miles one way
Elevation gain: 2,050 feet
High point: 5,050 feet
Allow 3½ hours one way
Usually open late June through October
Topographic maps:
U.S.G.S. Badger Lake, Oreg.
7.5'   1962
U.S.G.S. Dog River, Oreg.
7.5'   1962

The expanse of Elk Meadows is the terminus of the Cold Spring Creek Trail and this huge grassy clearing below the east face of Mt. Hood is an enchanting place for an extended rest after the long, but gradual, climb. From the Meadows you can hike 1.2 miles to the Timberline Trail and head west or north along this route that encircles Mt. Hood.

The Cold Spring Creek Trail follows the western base of Bluegrass Ridge and you could return along the crest of this ridge, rejoining the main trail at 2.7 miles. This loop would add about three-quarters mile and 600 feet of elevation gain (see No. 36). You also could return along the 2.5 mile long trail from Hood River Meadows Campground (No. 37) but this would involve a car shuttle.

Drive on Oregon 35 for 14.5 miles east and north of the junction of US 26 and Oregon 35 or 25.5 miles south of Hood River to a large parking area off the west side of the highway where a sign states East Fork Trail No. 650. This turnout is one-quarter mile north of Sherwood Campground and one mile south of Polallie Campground.

The trail begins from the northwest edge of the turnout at a sign and winds through woods for a few hundred feet to a narrow footbridge across the East Fork of the Hood River. Hike parallel to the river and the highway for 0.4 mile, traveling at a gradual uphill grade, to the edge of the canyon formed by Cold Spring Creek.

Turn sharply west and traverse for 150 yards to the junction of a trail from Polallie Campground. Keep left (straight), descend slightly and cross Cold Spring Creek on a footbridge. Climb moderately along the north bank of the creek, periodically passing through some brief swampy areas. Near the edge of a boulder field at 1.4 miles switchback right and after a short distance come to the junction of the 0.2 mile long spur to the viewpoint near the base of Tamanawaus Falls (No. 33).

Turn right, after a few yards pass a pipe on your left and continue traversing uphill. Curve left and come to the crest of a ridge at the junction of a second trail to Polallie Campground. Turn left and walk at a gentle grade along the broad, wooded crest then climb slightly to the unmarked junction of a trail to a jeep road that connects with the Cloud Cap Road. Keep left and resume climbing, passing through a semi-open area where you can see the intermontane valley that separates Oregon 35 from the main slopes of Mt. Hood. Drop slightly and come to the signed junction of Trail No. 644. Originally, this route was to have ended at Lamberson Butte but construction was halted after three miles. Keep left and pass a sign indicating you are on Trail No. 645. Hike downhill and come to the junction of the Bluegrass Ridge Trail. If you make the possible loop you will be returning along this route.

Keep right and cross a stream on a small bridge then climb at an easy grade. At 3.4 miles come near the North Fork of Cold Spring Creek and cross it on a foot log. Continue climbing moderately, with a few level stretches, through the forest. Near 6.0 miles the grade becomes increasingly more gradual and eventually levels off. Come to the northern edge of Elk Meadows, cross a stream and reach the wooden shelter and many campsites.

Elk Meadows

Trail across Cold Spring Creek

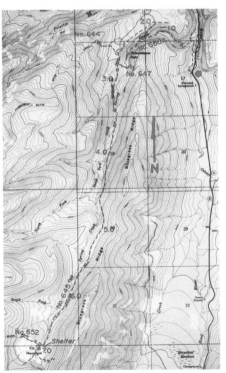

36 BLUEGRASS RIDGE

One day trip or backpack
Distance: 7.8 miles one way
Elevation gain: 2,780 feet; loss 700 feet
High point: 5,700 feet
Allow 3½ to 4 hours one way
Usually open July through October
Topographic maps:
  U.S.G.S. Badger Lake, Oreg.
  7.5'   1962
  U.S.G.S. Dog River, Oreg.
  7.5'   1962

Bluegrass Ridge

This trail traverses almost the entire length of five mile long Bluegrass Ridge then winds down to Elk Meadows. You probably will want to spend a considerable amount of time at the destination lounging on the grass, enjoying the view of Newton Clark Glacier on the east face of Mt. Hood and investigating the Meadow, the largest on the slopes of the peak. You can see some new scenery and save 0.7 mile of hiking and 500 feet of elevation gain by returning along the Cold Spring Creek Trail (No. 35). Also, by establishing a car shuttle, you could return along the 2.5 mile long Elk Meadows Trail (No. 37).

Drive on Oregon 35 for 14.5 miles east and north of the junction of US 26 and Oregon 35 or 25.5 miles south of Hood River to a large parking area off the west side of the highway where a sign states East Fork Trail No. 650. This turnout is ¼ mile north of Sherwood Campground and 1.0 mile south of Polallie Campground.

The trail begins from the northwest edge of the turnout at a sign and winds through woods for a few hundred feet to a narrow footbridge across the East Fork of the Hood River. Hike parallel to the river and the highway for 0.4 mile, generally traveling at a gradual uphill grade, to the edge of the canyon formed by Cold Spring Creek. Turn sharply west for 150 yards to the junction of a trail from Polallie Campground. Keep left (straight), descend slightly and cross Cold Spring Creek on a footbridge. Climb erratically, but always moderately, beside the creek. Near the edge of a boulder field at 1.4 miles switchback right and after a short distance come to the junction of the 0.2 mile spur to Tamanawaus Falls (No. 33).

Turn right, after a few yards pass a pipe on your left and continue traversing uphill. Curve left and come to the crest of a ridge at the junction of a second trail to Polallie Campground. Turn left and walk at a gentle grade along the broad, wooded crest then climb slightly to an unmarked junction. Keep left, resume climbing then drop slightly and come to the signed junction of Trail No. 644. Keep left again and hike downhill to the junction of the Bluegrass Ridge Trail.

Turn left, drop slightly then climb over a low hump. Cross a small stream just before coming to the North Fork of Cold Spring Creek. If the planned bridge has not been constructed, you may be able to cross on a large log several yards upstream. Climb steeply then more moderately up the northwest end of Bluegrass Ridge to the crest and begin the four mile traverse along the mostly wooded ridge top. The generally moderate uphill grade occasionally is interrupted by brief stretches of downhill. Near 5.9 miles the route leaves the crest and traverses the east side of the slope for 1.1 miles.

Where you rejoin the ridge top at 7.0 miles you can backtrack along the summit to a rocky viewpoint. Come to the junction of the trail to Elk Mountain (see No. 37), keep right and begin winding steeply downhill for one-third mile. Stay along the left (south) edge of the first open area then at a second, larger clearing follow the route marked by a few stakes. Intersect the trail from Hood River Meadows Campground, turn right and walk the short distance to the shelter.

Mt. Hood from Elk Meadows

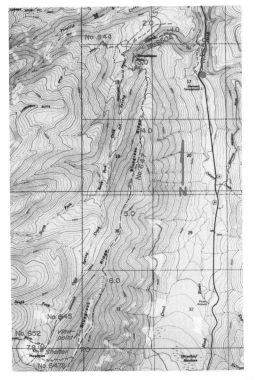

37 ELK MEADOWS and LAMBER-
SON BUTTE

One day trip or backpack
Distance: 4.5 miles one way
Elevation gain: 2,155 feet
High point: 6,633 feet
Allow 3 to 4 hours one way
Usually open mid-July through mid-October
Topographic maps:
   U.S.G.S. Badger Lake, Oreg.
   7.5'   1962
   U.S.G.S. Timberline Lodge, Oreg.
   7.5'   1962

Elk Meadows is the largest meadow on the slopes of Mt. Hood — the immense, grassy clearing, with its quaint wooden shelter and the superb view of the east face of the peak, is a fine stopping place for backpackers or for hikers who do not want to complete the trip along Gnarl Ridge to the spectacular view of Newton Clark Glacier from Lamberson Butte. An optional loop that would add 2.5 miles and 350 feet of elevation gain can be made to Elk Mountain located southeast of the meadow.

Drive on Oregon 35 to the road to Mt. Hood Meadows Ski Area located 6.5 miles east of the junction of US 26 and Oregon 35 and 33.5 miles south of Hood River. Turn west and after several yards turn right onto the old Mt. Hood Loop Highway and proceed 1.2 miles to the entrance to Hood River Meadows Campground where a sign states Elk Meadows. Turn left, after a few yards keep right where the road forks then 150 feet farther come to the north end of the loop through the campground and park your car along the spur that continues straight ahead. If all the spaces here are taken you can turn left and drive along the loop road to the campground where more parking is available. A sign stating Elk Meadows Trail and listing several mileages a few yards along the spur identifies the beginning of the hike.

Walk along the spur road that soon narrows into a trail and hike at a gradual grade through woods to the footbridge over Clark Creek at 0.5 mile. Cross Kate and Warren Creeks and at 1.0 mile come to the junction of the Newton Creek Trail that heads northwest to the Timberline Trail. Keep straight (right) and soon make an easy crossing of Newton Creek on a huge log. Traverse uphill and climb in a series of switchbacks then continue at a more gradual grade to the junc-

tion at 2.1 miles of the Bluegrass Ridge Trail to Elk Mountain. If you plan to go directly to Elk Meadows keep straight (left), walk for several hundred yards to the edge of the clearing and continue through the meadow to the shelter cabin near the northeastern corner.

To make the side loop to Elk Mountain turn right and climb moderately, pass through an open area along the crest then drop slightly and come to a junction. After visiting Elk Mountain you will be following the trail that goes left here. Note features of the terrain between here and the summit as the route is easy to lose on the return. Keep right and walk at a gradual grade to the site of the former lookout. To complete the loop, return to the junction of No. 647, descend slightly then traverse uphill along the east side of a sparsely wooded slope. Follow the faint path over the crest and after several yards come to a junction. Turn left and descend steeply through woods for one-third mile to the western edge of the meadow. Continue toward the center of the clearing until you intersect the Elk Meadows Trail and turn right.

To complete the hike to Gnarl Ridge and Lamberson Butte follow the path, marked by poles, that heads northwest from the shelter. Enter woods and climb moderately for 1.0 mile to the junction with the Timberline Trail. Turn right and travel up through woods and periodic grassy areas. Just before 4.0 miles begin traversing along the rocky, less vegetated northern slope of the ridge. Pass the remains of a stone shelter to your left above the trail and come to a flat, open area of bush-like, gnarled white bark pine that affords an excellent stopping place and viewpoint. To reach Lamberson Butte, climb to the southeast for several hundred yards.

Trail sign

On Gnarl Ridge

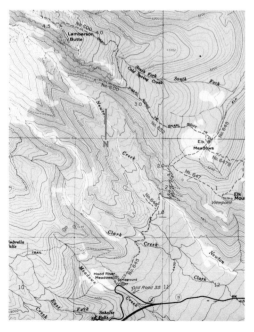

38 LOOKOUT MOUNTAIN

One day trip
Distance: 5.6 miles one way
Elevation gain: 2,925 feet
High point: 6,525 feet
Allow 4 hours one way
Usually open late June through October
Topographic map:
    U.S.G.S. Badger Lake, Oreg.
    7.5'   1962

The original structure on Lookout Mountain was a log cabin built in 1908. The site was an excellent choice for spotting fires as the view from the summit is one of the most extensive in the Mt. Hood area: Mounts Jefferson and Washington, the Three Sisters, Broken Top and the tips of The Husband and Bachelor Butte rise to the south and Paulina Crater, Smith Rocks, Tygh Valley and the town of Madras are a few of the landmarks to the southeast. The outline of the Blue Mountains forms the eastern horizon and closer by to the north and northeast are Mounts St. Helens, Rainier and Adams, the Columbia River, John Day Dam and Upper and Lower Hood River Valleys. Badger Lake (No. 39) can be seen in a depression two miles to the south and Mt. Hood fills the scene to the west.

In the lush meadow three-quarters mile from the summit you can examine the remains of a guard station that was constructed about the same time as the first summit cabin. Although long range plans by the Forest Service include rebuilding the original trail to the summit, currently the middle two miles of the hike are along a dirt road that affords continual views of the east face of Mt. Hood. Begin the hike with a full bottle of water as the one source along the hike may not be dependable.

Proceed on Oregon 35 for 10.5 miles east and north of its junction with US 26 or approximately 29.5 miles south of Hood River to a large sign stating Gumjuwac Saddle on the east side of the highway about 100 yards south of Robin Hood Campground. Turn east, cross the East Fork of the Hood River and come to the trail head and a large parking area at the north end of a gravel pit.

Traverse north along the wooded slope for 0.1 mile, meet the old trail that begins several hundred yards north along the highway, keep right and begin climbing at a steady, moderate grade in a series of switchbacks. At 1.3 miles begin a short traverse then switchback right and come near the rim of a rocky crest. Switchback left across a small scree area then travel in woods for a short distance to a good view of Mt. Hood. Climb near the rocky edge before continuing uphill along the wooded slope. Pass Jack Springs just below the trail and go the final several hundred yards to Road S21 at Gumjuwac Saddle. The route to Badger Lake crosses the road and descends east.

Turn left, walk up the road and 0.4 mile from Gumjuwac Saddle pass a helispot on the grassy crest to your right. The route of the proposed Lookout Mountain Trail will follow the ridge northeast from here. Continue the gradual climb along the road then begin curving to the northeast near 3.8 miles and come to the edge of High Prairie. Walk on the level for 0.2 mile to a four-way junction and turn right as indicated by the sign pointing to Lookout Mountain.

Continue at a gradual grade through a woods of widely spaced trees and grass. Note where an old road comes in from the left so you do not accidentally follow it on your return. About 0.3 mile from the junction be watching for the remnants of the former log guard station on your left. Enter deeper woods at the south end of the meadow and climb in switchbacks at a very moderate grade to a saddle. From here you can go cross-country to interesting rock outcroppings along the south side of the crest. Continue along the road and just before it curves left to the summit pass a sign identifying the Divide Trail to Oval Lake and Flag Point.

Old guard station at High Prairie

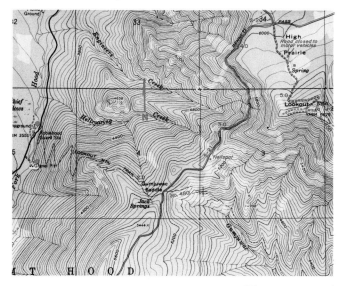

39 BADGER LAKE

One day trip or backpack
Distance: 6.5 miles one way
Elevation gain: 2,195 feet; loss 1,320 feet
High point: 5,220 feet
Allow 4 hours one way
Usually open July through October
Topographic map:
   U.S.G.S. Badger Lake, Oreg.
   7.5'   1962

Time out at Gumjuwac Creek

Badger Lake is one of the largest in the Mt. Hood area and the trail to it climbs over Gumjuwac Saddle then drops through meadows and woods before reaching its northwestern shore. Views enjoyed along the hike include the east side of Mt. Hood and the treeless terrain surrounding Tygh Valley. Although presently a road, S340, goes to the northeastern shore of Badger Lake, long range plans of the Forest Service call for its eventual closure to motor vehicles.

Drive on Oregon 35 for 10.5 miles north and east of its junction with US 26 or approximately 29.5 miles south of Hood River to a large sign stating Gumjuwac Saddle on the east side of the highway about 100 yards south of Robin Hood Campground. Turn east, cross the East Fork of the Hood River and come to the trailhead and parking area at the north end of a gravel pit.

Traverse north along the wooded slope for 0.1 mile, meet the old trail to Gumjuwac Saddle that begins several hundred yards north along the highway, keep right and begin climbing at a steady, moderate grade in a series of irregular switchbacks. As you gain elevation you will have glimpses of Mt. Hood. At 1.3 miles begin traversing along the southwestern slope of a large side canyon. Switchback right and come near the rim of a rocky crest then turn left and cross a small scree area. Traverse in woods for a short distance, switchback and come to a good view of Mt. Hood. Climb near the rocky edge of the slope for a short distance then continue uphill at a moderate grade. Pass Jack Springs that may not flow all summer just below the trail and continue the final several hundred yards to Road S21. A large sign here marks Gumjuwac Saddle and relates the story of the unusual name. The route to Lookout Mountain (No. 38) continues left up the road.

Cross the road then traverse down through woods for a few hundred feet to a large meadow where you will have a view east toward the Tygh Valley area. Descend steeply through the clearing for a couple hundred feet then continue downhill, veering left, at a more moderate grade. The path becomes faint for a short distance so note landmarks to facilitate your return. Reenter woods where a blaze has been cut on a tree and resume traveling on an obvious tread. Descend along the slope of trees and small, grassy clearings and cross a stream. The moderate grade is interrupted at one point by a couple hundred feet of steep downhill. Come to a larger side stream at 3.5 miles that is a good place for a snack stop.

Continue down through denser woods to the junction of the Badger Creek Trail at 4.2 miles. Keep straight (right) and ford Gumjuwac Creek. Climb gradually through woods, crossing several small side streams, and two miles from the junction come to an unsigned fork and keep left. Pass a trail on your right and come to a large sign and a junction. The trail to the left goes to Road S340 and the campground. Keep straight (right) and walk on the level for 0.1 mile to a large sign. The main trail continues to Road S339 east of Camp Windy. Turn left and walk for 100 feet to a grassy section of the lake shore.

Aerial view of Badger Lake

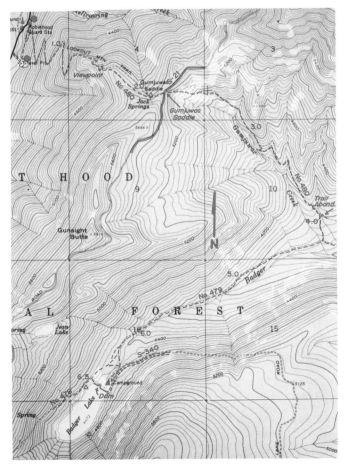

40 HUCKLEBERRY MOUNTAIN

One day trip
Distance: 4.5 miles one way
Elevation gain: 3,070 feet; loss 100 feet
High point: 4,250 feet
Allow 3 to 3½ hours one way
Usually open mid-May through November
Topographic map:
  U.S.G.S. Rhododendron, Oreg.
  7.5'   1962

The climb to the viewpoint at 4.5 miles on the rocky summit ridge of Huckleberry Mountain is a good choice for people who want both a strenuous hike and a destination where they can relax and enjoy an extensive view. The southwest side of Mt. Hood fills the scene to the northeast and visible between it and Mt. Jefferson and Olallie Butte to the south are Hunchback, Lookout and Tom Dick Mountains, Devils Peak and Salmon Butte. By establishing a car shuttle you can return along the trail that winds down the east side of Huckleberry Mountain. This optional return would add no additional distance or elevation gain. Also, a trail continues beyond the viewpoint and after 2.5 miles joins the trail to Wildcat Mountain. No water is available beyond 0.5 miles.

Proceed on US 26 to Arrah Wanna Boulevard 0.5 mile west of Wemme, a community 17.0 miles east of Sandy and 1.0 miles west of Zigzag. Turn south and drive 0.9 mile to a bridge over the Salmon River. At the south end of the span turn right and go 0.1 mile to a sign on your left indicating the beginning of the Arrah Wanna Trail. Parking spaces are available for a few cars. (If you are establishing a car shuttle, first drive on US 26 to the Hoodland Shopping Center, 0.5 mile east of Arrah Wanna Boulevard and 1.0 mile west of Zigzag. Turn south, pass a golf course and 1.3 miles from the highway keep right at a fork in the road. Continue 0.1 mile to a bridge over the Salmon River and at the west end of the span turn right and follow a private road a short distance to its end where a sign marks the beginning of the Plaza Trail. Parking space is limited here.)

Climb moderately through dense woods of second growth deciduous trees. Cross a few small streams that may not flow all summer and continue uphill at a moderately steep grade. The route veers right and crosses an old overgrown logging road and the angle of the trail becomes more moderate. Two-tenths mile from the roadbed cross two forks of a stream, the last sources of water. After 150 yards the trail begins switchbacking and the grade increases considerably. Continue climbing in very short switchbacks interspersed with a few brief traverses. At the end of the switchbacks come to a crest and a short path to a forested knob.

Keep left on the main trail and descend along the crest to a wooded saddle at 1.9 miles. Resume climbing and eventually begin winding steeply uphill in short, loose switchbacks. Climb on the top of a ridge for a few hundred feet then begin winding up along or near the crest at a very steep grade through increasingly numerous rhododendron bushes. The grade soon becomes more moderate and after a slight drop the route travels on the level to the junction of the Plaza Trail. If you make the loop you will be returning along the trail to your left.

Turn right and climb briefly then travel on the level before descending slightly. Walk on the level again then climb and drop once more before the final uphill stretch to the viewpoint. Ground-hugging phlox are plentiful along the open crest in the early spring.

To return along Trail No. 783 keep right at the junction at 3.0 miles and switchback down through dense timber. Begin traversing in a northerly direction 2.2 miles from the crest and cross a few small rocky stream beds near the end of the trail.

Wild iris on the Arrah Wanna Trail

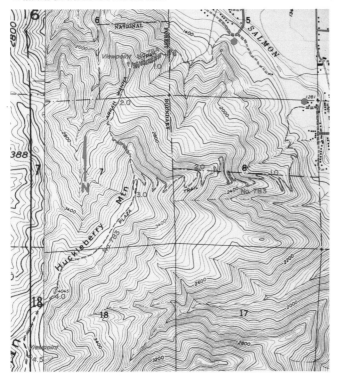

41 HUNCHBACK MOUNTAIN

One day trip
Distance: 4.5 miles one way
Elevation gain: 2,820 feet; loss 210 feet
High point: 4,033 feet
Allow 3 to 4 hours one way
Usually open June through November
Topographic map:
   U.S.G.S. Rhododendron, Oreg.
   7.5'   1962

The frequently steep climb along the western end of the massive, wooded ridge extending from the Salmon River to Still Creek passes several impressive viewpoints. The first is a narrow, precipitous and rocky crest 1,800 feet above Welches golf course and resort and another is reached by scrambling over a boulder field for a few hundred feet. During late September a great variety of mushrooms poke through the forest floor or cling to decaying logs. Be sure to carry an adequate supply of water as none is available along the hike.

Although the text describes only the first 4.5 miles of the hike, the trail continues another 4.5 miles to Devils Peak, so you could do the trip as a loop by returning along No. 54. The circuit would be a total of 13 miles, add 1,600 feet of elevation gain and necessitate a short car shuttle.

Drive on US 26 18 miles east of Sandy to the Zigzag Ranger Station on the south side of the highway across from the Lolo Pass Road and park at the east end of the large parking area.

Walk east from the parking area along an old road for a few hundred feet to a sign identifying the beginning of the Hunchback Trail. Turn right and walk 25 yards to another old road bed. Cross it and after several feet turn left near a small building and begin a noticeable climb. After a hundred yards switchback right just before a cistern that affords water for a face wash on the return and continue traversing, but at a more moderate grade. Make two more short switchbacks then traverse around the west face of the slope. Switchback left and cross a bench. For the next mile climb in a series of switchbacks and traverses then near 1.6 miles travel at a more moderate grade and follow a crest for a short distance before traversing downhill to a saddle. Wend your way around a few rocks on the crest then resume climbing

steeply and at 2.2 miles come to the exposed view down over the golf course and beyond to the wooded terrain comprising the Salmon River drainage.

Drop slightly, reenter woods and climb at an erratic grade. Keep right at an unofficial sign marking a path down to a Girl Scout Camp and climb steeply for about 200 feet to a sign identifying the route to viewpoint rockpile. To reach the crest, turn right and follow the short path to the edge of a boulder field. Look up to the skyline and locate a clump of vine maple with a Douglas fir snag on the right. Scramble up and over the large boulders, aiming for this vegetation. A path leads left between the maple and the fir to a cluster of boulders on the crest. A small sign identifies Washbowl Rock.

The main trail traverses at a moderate grade for several yards, passing an open area that affords a few of Mt. Hood, then resumes climbing steeply. Wind up beside the western edge of a small boulder field then curve left and cross the scree. Climb moderately then soon begin walking along a broad, almost level section of the crest. Eventually, the ridge narrows and near 3.6 miles the route passes a sign stating Viewpoint-Helispot. The main trail begins to descend along the east slope of the ridge. Periodically, the grade is level or uphill for short distances. Follow along the crest for one-quarter mile then where the trail switchbacks down to the left, keep straight for about 150 feet to reach the viewpoint at 4.5 miles. The main trail continues downhill, losing 400 feet of elevation, then goes uphill for four miles to Devils Peak.

Spider web across trail

Washbowl Rock

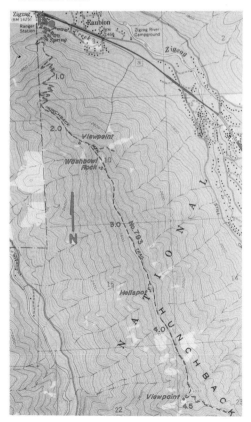

42 OLD SALMON RIVER TRAIL

One-half day trip
Distance: 2.6 miles one way
Elevation gain: 100 feet
High point: 1,640 feet
Allow 1½ hours one way
Usually open late February through December
Topographic map:
  U.S.G.S. Rhododendron, Oreg.
  7.5'   1962

A trail once paralleled the Salmon River all the way from the community of Welches to Government Camp but the construction of Road S38 disrupted portions of the first four miles of the original route. However, this northernmost section of the Old Salmon River Trail still provides 2½ miles of easy, scenic hiking. Although S38 is glimpsed several times during the hike and the route actually follows the road twice for a few hundred yards, the deep lush woods and the constant proximity of the rushing Salmon River usually create the effect of being far from civilization. For the return portion of the hike you can retrace your steps, establish a car shuttle or hike back along the road.

Proceed 17¾ miles east of Sandy on US 26 or ¼ mile west of Zigzag to the Salmon River Road, S38, and turn south. Drive 2.6 miles and 500 feet beyond the boundary of the Mount Hood National Forest come to a sign on the west side of the road marking the beginning of the hike. If you plan to establish a car shuttle, continue 2.5 miles farther along S38 and park by the first bridge across the Salmon River.

Descend gradually through moss-encrusted woods, periodically climbing very slightly. Cross a small stream and continue hiking through the rain forest. Although the evergreens are not especially close together, the hanging moss and the carpet of ferns create a dense, lush environment. Travel parallel to the Salmon River and come to a more open area where sorrel, larkspur and other wild flowers bloom during early spring. At 0.5 mile cross a former bed of the Salmon River then curve away from the main flow and recross the old bed. Climb the steep bank and resume walking in a southerly direction. Cross a partially collapsed bridge near 0.8 mile and after traversing along the bank come to a junction a few hundred feet

to a campsite near a place in the river where the flow of water is slowed by a deep hole.

Bear left to stay on the main route and continue through woods. Near 1.0 mile the trail widens into a faint, old roadbed. Keep right on a path and after a few hundred feet meet a more obvious, but abandoned, old vehicle way and keep straight. Cross a wide, shallow stream and a short distance farther be watching for and follow a path that veers to the right and is marked by swaths of blue paint sprayed on tree trunks.

At 1.4 miles meet Road S38 and walk along its shoulder for 0.1 mile for the length of a rock retaining wall. In many of the sunny areas along the roadbed coltsfoot thrive and the cluster of cream-colored blossoms at the end of the thick stalks are easy to identify. Immediately at the end of the reinforcement drop again to river level. (The resumption of the trail is unmarked.) Soon reenter a mossy woods and follow the winding trail near the river. Where you come near the road stay right along the edge of the bank. Come to the northwestern edge of Green Canyon Campground at 2.0 miles and keep right near the bank. Pass many picnic tables and benches and a short distance beyond the south end climb several yards to the road. Walk along the shoulder for 100 yards then descend along the obvious path that leaves the road at a shallow angle. Continue through woods for 0.3 mile to the end of the hike at S38 where a bridge spans the Salmon River. The remainder of the trail along the Salmon River (No. 44) resumes across the pavement.

Salmon River

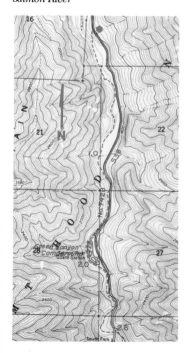

43 SALMON BUTTE

One day trip
Distance: 4.3 miles one way
Elevation gain: 2,800 feet
High point: 4,877 feet
Allow 2½ to 3½ hours one way
Usually open June through October
Topographic maps:
    U.S.G.S. High Rock, Oreg.
    15'   1956
    U.S.G.S. Rhododendron, Oreg.
    7.5'   1962

Sorrel blossom

The climb to the rocky, treeless summit of Salmon Butte is one of the most scenic and enjoyable of the trips in the foothills south of Mt. Hood. The route generally travels through woods of varying, but always attractive, character until reaching the top where the view extends from Mounts St. Helens, Adams and Rainier along the northern horizon, over landmarks in the Columbia River Gorge and past the southwest face of Mt. Hood to Mt. Jefferson on the southern skyline. In mid-July your progress through the clearcut at the beginning of the hike may be slowed by the abundance of succulent, tiny wild blackberries. Fill your water bottle before leaving home as the sources along the trail may not be dependable all season.

Drive on US 26 to the Salmon River Road located 17¾ miles east of Sandy and one-quarter mile west of the community of Zigzag and turn south. Proceed 5.2 miles, cross a bridge over the Salmon River and 0.6 mile farther cross another span. One and one-tenth miles from the second one come to a logging spur on your right where a sign identifies the beginning of the Salmon Butte Trail. Parking spaces are available along the shoulder of the main road.

Walk up the logging spur for about 100 yards and just before the end of the roadbed be looking to your left for the numbers 791 spray painted on two tree trunks. Turn left here and follow the path up through the clearcut. The formal trail begins from the edge of the woods at the southern, upper end of the logged area and climbs moderately through the deep forest. At 1.0 mile cross the face of a ridge and travel through less lush woods for a few hundred feet to the junction of an unmaintained trail to Mack Hall Creek. Keep left and 0.2 mile farther come to a viewpoint at a small, open rocky area. Reenter woods and continue traversing. At 1.7 miles hop over a small side stream then cross the face of another ridge. Make two short switchbacks and come to a second possible water source. Continue traversing then make three switchbacks of varying lengths and at 2.9 miles abruptly cross to the east side of the summit ridge.

After 200 feet come to an open area that affords a view of the southwest face of Mt. Hood. Reenter woods and begin climbing along a narrow portion of the crest. The ridge broadens and the trail passes a third possible water source. Traverse through a brushy area then curve right and make one switchback through a timbered slope with no ground cover. Climb through a patch of rhododendron bushes, wind up for several yards and come to Road S409. Turn right and follow the road as it winds around the summit cone of Salmon Butte for 0.2 mile to its end just below the site of the former lookout cabin. In addition to the major peaks, you can identify lesser highpoints such as Silver Star Mountain in Washington, Larch and Chinidere Mountains, Palmer and Tanner Buttes and Mt. Defiance in the Columbia River Gorge, Wildcat Mountain and Devils Peak nearby to the west and east and Signal and Olallie Buttes to the south.

Mt. Hood from Salmon Butte

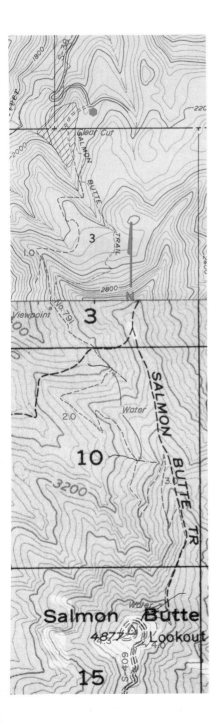

44 SALMON RIVER TRAIL

One day trip
Distance: 3.7 miles one way to (second
Viewpoint)
Elevation gain: 890 feet; loss 400 feet
(to second Viewpoint)
High point: 2,490 feet
Allow 2 to 2½ hours one way
Usually open March through December
Topographic map:
  U.S.G.S. Rhododendron, Oreg.
  7.5'   1962

Salmon River canyon

The Salmon River Trail is the continuation of the Old Salmon River Trail described in No. 42 and parallels the robust stream for 14 miles before veering north and ending at a logging spur 5.5 miles from Government Camp. A use-path descends from the main trail at 3.5 miles to a steep, grassy slope that affords a good stopping place and a fine view of Final and Frustration Falls. During late May the blossoms of columbine, larkspur, penstemon, Indian paintbrush and other gay wild flowers add color to the predominant greens of the mosses, ferns and trees along the route and as the trail gains elevation the woods are sprinkled in early June with the delicate pink blooms of the rhododendron.

Carry water in late summer as the several small streams along the route may not be dependable all year. Because of its relatively low elevation, the hike can be done earlier and later in the season than most of the other trips in the Mt. Hood area.

Proceed on US 26 to a sign marking the Salmon River Road on the south side of the highway 17¾ miles east of Sandy and one-quarter mile west of the community of Zig-zag. Turn south and follow the road for 5.2 miles to a large bridge over the Salmon River where a sign on the east shoulder just before the span marks the trailhead. Parking for cars is available off both sides of the road.

Climb for a short distance then travel with brief ups and downs through lush woods. The route vascillates between traveling beside the Salmon River and several hundred feet from the water's edge. At 1.7 miles pass through Big Horn Campground then walk through woods at a gradual grade and 0.5 mile farther come to Rolling Riffle Campground. Continue on the level for a short distance then begin climbing away from the river along the slope of Douglas

fir and rhododendron bushes. Near 3.2 miles where the trail switchbacks left, keep straight and traverse the open, grassy slope to a fine view of the narrow, rocky gorge formed by the Salmon River. This is a scenic place to end the hike if you do not want to visit the viewpoint 0.5 mile farther.

Return to the main trail and continue climbing through woods. Hike in and out of a side canyon and traverse across the face of a broad ridge. Where the trail levels off and begins to descend look right for an unmarked, well-defined path heading downslope. Turn right and descend through the woods for about 100 feet then where the slope becomes steep turn right. Drop steeply for a short distance then curve left and contour around the ridge crest. Hike down the grassy, open crest, bearing slightly left, until you can see Final and Frustration Falls cascading down the steep, rocky wall to the east. A good spot for lunch is downslope on the grassy bench.

Rain forest near the Salmon River

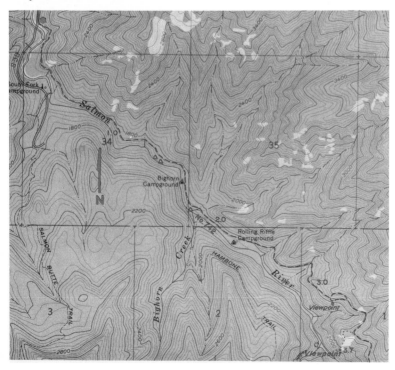

45 CASTLE CANYON

One-half day trip
Distance: 0.9 miles one way
Elevation gain: 850 feet
High point: 2,450 feet
Allow 45 minutes to 1 hour one way
Usually open March through November
Topographic map:
   U.S.G.S. Rhododendron, Oreg.
   7.5'   1962

Castle Canyon was named for the spire-shaped outcroppings of alluvial conglomerate protruding above the wooded southern slope of West Zigzag Mountain between the 1,800 and 2,800 foot levels. Some geologists think this area once was a lateral moraine of the Zigzag Glacier. Although the hike through this interesting region is less than one mile in length, the path climbs very steeply for most of its distance. Carry water as none is available along the way.

Drive 18 miles east of Sandy on US 26 to the Lolo Pass Road at the community of Zigzag, turn north and drive 0.4 mile to a road on your right identified as "19". Turn right, keep straight (right) at a fork after 0.2 mile and continue 1.4 miles to a sign on your left stating Castle Canyon Trail. Park along the shoulder of the road. Since Road 19 continues to Rhododendron, two miles east of Zigzag, you do not need to turn your car around. (If you are approaching from the east, drive to the west end of Rhododendron and turn north at small signs stating Henry Creek Road and Little Brook Lane then after a few yards turn left onto Henry Creek Road.

Go 0.3 mile to a fork, turn left onto Road 19 and drive 0.4 mile to the trailhead.

Climb gradually along a wooded slope that was selectively logged with draft horses. After a few hundred yards cross a narrow old roadbed and continue climbing moderately. Reach the end of the logged area and begin climbing more noticeably in short switchbacks. Continue winding up at an increasingly steeper grade and reach a ridge crest.

At 0.5 mile come to the first of the exposed rock. Continue up the narrow ridge crest then travel around the right side of an outcropping. Follow the path that climbs steeply along the eastern base of the high, rock wall. Just below a little saddle a side path goes right for 100 feet to a small notch overlooking more formations.

From the saddle climb very steeply for a few hundred feet to a crest. You can continue up the ridge for several hundred yards to a higher viewpoint if you wish. The site of the former lookout on West Zigzag Mountain can be seen above to the northeast and several populated areas along US 26 are visible to the southwest.

The Castles

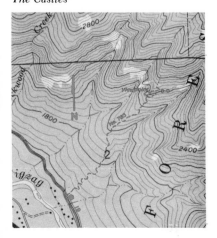

46 WEST ZIGZAG MOUNTAIN

One day trip
Distance: 5 miles one way
Elevation gain: 3,400 feet; loss 340 feet
High point: 4,525 feet
Allow 3 to 3½ hours one way
Usually open June through mid-November
Topographic map:
   U.S.G.S. Rhododendron, Oreg.
   7.5'   1962

Although West Zigzag Mountain and East Zigzag Mountain (see hike No. 49) are along the same major ridge, the two summits are over two miles apart and separated by Cast Mountain and a smaller, unnamed peak. A circuitous route connects the two Zigzag Mountains and by establishing a car shuttle you could make a long one-way trip. You also could follow Trail No. 774 that continues to the northeast to Horseshoe Ridge (No. 47), Cast Creek (No. 48) or Devils Meadow (No. 52) Trails. From the site of the former lookout cabin on the top of the cliff band near the summit of West Zigzag Mountain the view extends west down the Sandy River Valley toward Portland and the climb to this perch is a perfect choice when you want a moderately strenuous, easily accessible trip with good scenery. Carry water as none is available along the hike.

Proceed 18 miles east of Sandy on US 26 to the Lolo Pass Road at the community of Zigzag, turn north and drive 0.4 mile to a road on your right identified as "19". Turn right, keep straight (right) at a fork after 0.2 mile and continue 0.4 mile to a sign on your left that identifies the beginning of the Zigzag Mountain Trail and lists many mileages. A turnout east of the sign provides a few parking spaces. (If you are approaching from the east, drive to the west end of Rhododendron and turn north at small signs stating Henry Creek Road and Little Brook Lane then after a few yards turn left onto Henry Creek Road. After 0.3 mile come to a fork, turn left onto Road 19 and drive 1.4 miles to the trailhead.)

Traverse uphill for a short distance then begin a series of many switchbacks that climb for one mile at a steady, moderate grade along the wooded slope. Come to a viewpoint where you can see down onto Rhododendron and across to Hunchback Ridge and Devils Peak (No's. 41 and 54). Several yards farther come to the crest and climb along or just below it in traverses and switchbacks for the next 1.5 miles. Although erratic, the grade for the entire hike is always moderate. When not on the ridge top the trail goes along the east slope until 2.5 miles where it crosses to the west side. Switchback and resume traveling on the wall of the basin. Switchback twice more and make a long traverse. At 2.9 miles cross over the crest where you will be able to look north to the vicinity of Lolo Pass.

Hike along the crest in a series of short ups and downs, climbing steeply for one brief stretch, then make three short switchbacks and resume traversing. Walk along a less densely vegetated portion of the crest and come to a good view of Mt. Hood. Drop slightly, travel on the crest then along the north side of the slope and begin a gradual descent. Come to a saddle at 4.1 miles where you can see your destination at the top of the high cliffs to the southeast.

Continue dropping gradually along the crest then curve left and enter deeper woods. Switchback right and come to a treeless viewpoint. Wind up the open slope in several short switchbacks then resume hiking along the north side of the slope. Traverse above a little basin then begin descending gradually. Drop steeply for about 150 feet, curve left and walk along the base of a sheer rock wall. Climb in a couple of very short switchbacks then walk gradually downhill for a few hundred feet to where the trail curves sharply left. Turn right and drop for a few yards to reach the site of the former lookout.

Cliffs near site of the old lookout

47 HORSESHOE RIDGE

One day trip
Distance: 4 miles one way
Elevation gain: 2,210 feet
High point: 5,010 feet
Allow 2½ to 3 hours one way
Usually open July through October
Topographic map:
  U.S.G.S. Government Camp, Oreg.
  7.5'   1962

Zigzag Mountain is a five mile long ridge extending east from near the community of Zigzag. This hike climbs south along the crest of Horseshoe Ridge and meets the summit of Zigzag Mountain near its mid point. The trail continues another mile to Cast Mountain, one of the four high points along the crest of Zigzag Mountain. During the last 1.5 miles the route travels through an old burn and you will have unobstructed views of the southwestern side of Mt. Hood and the wooded terrain to the north. Carry water as none is available along the hike.

By establishing a short car shuttle or walking along Road S25D for 1.5 miles you can return along the Cast Creek Trail (No. 48). With a longer car shuttle you could hike back through Devils Meadow (No. 52) or climb to the northeast over East Zigzag Mountain and descend past Burnt Lake (No. 49). Also, you can head southwest from the 3.0 mile point and return along the trail over West Zigzag Mountain (No. 46).

Drive on US 26 to the community of Zigzag, 18 miles east of Sandy and two miles west of Rhododendron, and turn north on the Lolo Pass Road. Proceed 4.1 miles to a sign marking the road to McNeil Campground and turn right. Go downhill for 0.7 mile, turn right, cross a bridge and pass the entrance to McNeil Campground. One-half mile from the span turn right onto S25D at the sign indicating the route to Riley Campground and after 0.2 mile keep left at its en-trance. One and nine-tenths miles farther come to a sign identifying the beginning of the Horseshoe Ridge Trail.

Hike up through woods for 0.2 mile then begin a mile long series of moderately graded switchbacks. At 1.3 miles pass under a large rock outcropping and travel along the west side of the slope for a short distance. Make a few loose switchbacks then as the trail curves right near 2.0 miles stay on the main route where a faint, abandoned trail descends to Dumbbell Lake. Traverse a steep, wooded section of the slope and travel just below the crest then at 2.3 miles come to the ridge top where you will have an excellent view of Mt. Hood. Climb through sparse timber then travel along open slopes below the crest. Descend slightly to the junction of the Zigzag Mountain Trail at a wide saddle. From here you can see the summit of Cast Mountain.

Turn left and climb along the broad open crest. The beargrass (also called squawgrass and elkgrass) that covers the ground along the final mile usually bloom during July and its creamy-white, bulbous blossoms at the end of tall stalks are easy to identify. Where you come to a fork in the trail you can keep right if you want to by-pass the short side path up to the first viewpoint. Beyond this summit descend moderately to a wide saddle where you will have a glimpse of Dumbbell Lake then resume climbing the final 0.5 mile to the top of Cast Mountain and a view of Cast Lake.

Cast Lake

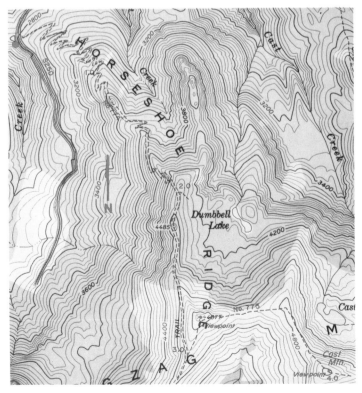

48 CAST CREEK TRAIL

One day trip or backpack
Distance: 4.5 miles one way
Elevation gain: 2,680 feet; loss 470 feet
High point: 4,600 feet
Allow 3 hours one way
Usually open July through October
Topographic maps:
    U.S.G.S. Bull Run Lake, Oreg.
    7.5'   1962
    U.S.G.S. Government Camp, Oreg.
    7.5'   1962

Trail signs near Cast Lake

Cast Lake lies below the northeastern end of the long ridge that forms Zigzag Mountain and the grassy shore is a good destination for both a one day hike and a backpack. Along much of the trip you will have unobstructed views of the southwest face of Mt. Hood and during July the thickets of rhododendron bushes along portions of the climb will be in bloom.

By establishing a base camp you can make side trips to Devils Meadow (No. 52), East Zigzag Mountain and Burnt Lake (No. 49), Cast Mountain and Horseshoe Ridge (No. 47) and West Zigzag Mountain (No. 46). With a car shuttle you can return along one of these trails and if you do not mind a 1.5 mile road walk you can follow the Horseshoe Ridge Trail without a shuttle. Carry water as none is available along the hike.

Proceed on US 26 to the community of Zigzag, 18 miles east of Sandy and two miles west of Rhododendron, and turn north on the Lolo Pass Road. Drive 4.1 miles to a sign marking the road to McNeil Campground and turn right. Go downhill for 0.7 mile, turn right, cross a bridge and pass the entrance to McNeil Campground. One-half mile from the span turn right onto S25D at the sign indicating the route to Riley Campground and after 0.2 mile keep left at its entrance. Four-tenths mile farther come to a post on the right side of the road. The trail, that may be unsigned, begins across the road from the post.

Climb steeply along the heavily wooded slope for 0.5 mile then hike a few hundred yards at a more moderate grade before curving right and resuming the more severe uphill grade. Come to the crest of the ridge at 0.9 mile and soon begin descending. Hike at an irregular grade with slight ups and downs and brief level stretches for 0.7 mile then resume climbing steeply for a short distance. The trail then levels off and you will have good views of the west face of Mt. Hood. Farther along the trail you also will be able to see Mounts Adams and St. Helens.

Resume climbing at 2.1 miles and travel through thickets of rhododendron bushes. Come to an almost treeless slope at 3.0 miles and reach the crest 0.1 mile farther. Rise moderately to a hump on the ridge top then descend slightly to a saddle. As you leave the crest keep right and continue downhill — do not follow the abandoned fire trail to East Zigzag Mountain. Drop for about 300 yards to a large, flat clearing and the junction of the Cast Lake Trail. To make the various side trips or loops mentioned in the second paragraph keep straight here.

Turn right and climb gradually over a low ridge then descend to the southern end of Cast Lake.

Mt. Hood from Cast Creek Trail

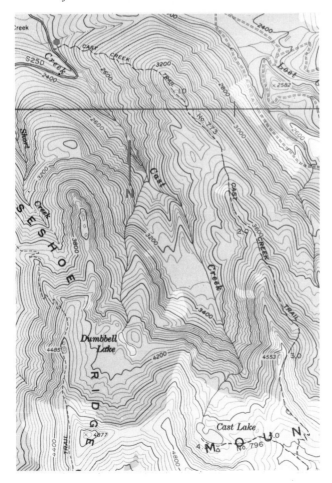

49 BURNT LAKE and EAST ZIGZAG MOUNTAIN

One day trip or backpack
Distance: 4 miles one way
Elevation gain: 2,320 feet
High point: 4,971 feet
Allow 3 to 3½ hours one way
Usually open June through October
Topographic map:
   U.S.G.S. Government Camp, Oreg.
   7.5'   1962

Burnt Lake is potentially one of the best swimming spots in the Mt. Hood area: the water is a pleasant temperature during late summer and the fine view of the southwest face of Mt. Hood is an added bonus. Although the lake is a completely satisfactory place to end the trip, the climb of East Zigzag Mountain to the west takes only about 30 minutes extra. From the summit, the most easterly point on the long ridge that forms Zigzag Mountain, you can see Burnt Lake and Mt. Hood, northwest into the Bull Run Reserve, west toward Portland, southeast toward the Ski Bowl at Government Camp and beyond to Mt. Jefferson. Between 2.0 and 2.5 miles the grade is very steep but the prospect of a swim or a long rest at the water's edge mitigates the effects of the climb.

Drive on US 26 to the community of Zigzag, 18 miles east of Sandy and two miles west of Rhododendron, and turn north on the Lolo Pass Road. Proceed 4.1 miles to a sign marking the road to McNeil Campground and Ramona Falls and turn right. Go downhill for 0.7 mile, turn right, cross a bridge and pass the entrance to McNeil Campground. One-half mile from the span keep straight and 1.2 miles farther turn right as indicated by the sign pointing to Burnt Lake Trail. Go 0.7 mile and just beyond Slide Creek keep straight (right) on S239G. Follow the road as it curves right then left and 0.9 mile from the start of S239G come to the end of the passable road in a large logged area where parking spaces are available for many cars. A sign identifying the start of the Burnt Lake Trail lists several mileages.

Walk along the old road that begins at the southeast corner of the parking area and follows the southern edge of the clearcut. After about 0.2 mile the road curves right and enters deep woods. Continue along the road for a short distance and where it curves slightly left be watching for a sign stating Burnt Lake Trail that marks a path heading off to the right. Turn right here and wind up moderately through attractive woods, keeping right where the trail forks. Continue up through the forest at an easy grade to a small stream crossing at 2.0 miles. Beyond the creek begin winding up very steeply for 0.6 mile then drop slightly and travel at a considerably more moderate grade for a short distance. Resume the ascent then climb less steeply and hike above a brushy clearing. Cross the outlet creek where you probably will see a crayfish or two. Climb steeply for one last stretch then pass just above the northwest shore of Burnt Lake. Where the trail forks near the eastern end keep left and wind down to a flat, grassy area near the water's edge.

To make the climb to the summit of East Zigzag Mountain, keep right at the fork above the east end of the lake, travel through a flat, marshy area then switchback up to the ridge crest. Keep right at the junction of the trail to Devils Meadow (No. 52) and Cast Lake (No. 48) and climb along the open ridge crest to the summit.

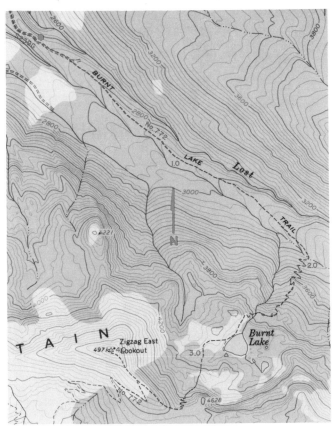

50 RAMONA FALLS LOOP

One day trip or backpack
Distance: 5.5 miles round trip
Elevation gain: 700 feet
High point: 3,450 feet
Allow 3 to 3½ hours round trip
Usually open April through November
Topographic map:
 U.S.G.S. Bull Run Lake, Oreg.
 7.5'   1962

For several good reasons, the Ramona Falls Loop is one of the most popular hikes in the Mt. Hood area: the elevation gain is minimal, the grade is gradual, both legs of the loop are scenic in their distinctive way and 100 foot high Ramona Falls is exceptionally attractive. The hike begins with a photogenic view of the west face of Mt. Hood then follows near the rim of the broad, severely eroded canyon formed by the Sandy River and returns through deep woods beside lovely Ramona Creek.

Proceed on US 26 to the community of Zigzag, 18 miles east of Sandy and two miles west of Rhododendron, and turn north on the Lolo Pass Road. Drive 4.1 miles to a sign marking the road to McNeil Campground and Ramona Falls and turn right. Go downhill for 0.7 mile, turn right, cross a bridge and pass the entrance to McNeil Campground. One-half mile from the span keep straight and 1.2 miles farther keep straight (left) again then continue on S25 the final 1.6 miles to the large parking area at the end of the road. An outbuilding is located southeast of the turnaround. Walk to the northeast end of the loop at the edge of the woods where a sign identifies the trailhead.

Walk several yards across the rocky, high-water stream bed to a high bridge over the Sandy River. The unusual design of the span was necessary because during periods of heavy runoff the river carries trees and other large debris and the supports of a lower, less heavily constructed bridge would be demolished. Turn right at the north end of the span and climb for a couple hundred feet to a junction. Turn right and walk at a gradual grade, descending slightly along one section. This level region, named Old Maid Flat, in the vicinity of the confluence of the Muddy Fork and the Sandy River is the result of a giant mudflow. In the fall it is a very popular area for mushroom harvesters. Occasionally, you can see former sections of the old trail that end abruptly where a portion of the slope has slipped. Much of this erosion occurred during the extremely high, violent flow of December, 1964.

At 1.9 miles come to the junction of the Pacific Crest Trail (see No. 59) and turn left. Climb to a picturesque stone shelter, the Upper Sandy Guard Station, and switchback right then left and traverse above the large cabin. Curve right and walk at a gradual grade for 0.2 mile. Pass a wooden, three-sided shelter on your right, enter deep woods and descend to Ramona Falls.

To complete the loop cross the creek near the base of the Falls on planks and after several yards come to the junction of the Yocum Ridge Trail (No. 51). Keep left and descend for 150 yards to a footbridge across Ramona Creek. Walk through deep, scenic woods at a slight downhill grade beside the stream. For the next mile a 100 foot high face of fractured rock towers above to the right. Recross Ramona Creek and continue parallel to the stream and wall. Near 4.1 miles veer away from the stream and hike through less dense woods of lodgepole pine. Come to the junction of Trail No. 600 (see No. 59), turn left, cross Ramona Creek for a fourth time and after a few hundred yards come to the junction at the beginning of the loop. Keep straight (right) and descend to the bridge.

Ramona Falls

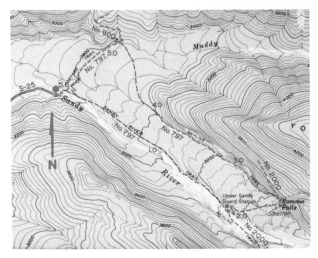

51 YOCUM RIDGE

One day trip
Distance: 7.6 miles one way
Elevation gain: 3,500 feet
High point: 6,200 feet
Allow 3½ to 4½ hours one way
Usually open late July through October
Topographic maps:
    U.S.G.S. Bull Run Lake, Oreg.
    7.5'   1962
    U.S.G.S. Cathedral Ridge, Oreg.
    7.5'   1962

A few hikes in the Mt. Hood area may equal the scenery enjoyed along the climb of Yocum Ridge but none can surpass it. If the weather is marginal consider doing another trip and save Yocum Ridge for a perfect day. Dominating the view is the west face of Mt. Hood and on a warm, sunny afternoon you probably will hear the awesome, momentarily terrifying, sound of a crumbling ice block on one of the several glaciers. The very steep use-path that formerly rose to the highest viewpoint was replaced in 1973 by a well-graded trail.

Drive on US 26 to the community of Zigzag, 18 miles east of Sandy and two miles west of Rhododendron, and turn north on the Lolo Pass Road. Proceed 4.1 miles to a sign marking the road to McNeil Campground and Ramona Falls and turn right. Go downhill for 0.7 mile, turn right, cross a bridge and pass the entrance to McNeil Campground. One-half mile from the span keep straight and 1.2 miles farther keep straight (left) again then continue on S25

the final 1.6 miles to the large parking area at the end of the road. An outhouse is located southeast of the turnaround. Walk to the northeast end of the loop at the edge of the woods where a sign identifies the trailhead.

Walk several yards to a high bridge over the Sandy River, turn right at the north end of the span and climb for a couple hundred feet to a junction. Turn right and generally walk at a gradual grade, descending slightly along one section. At 1.9 miles come to the junction of the Pacific Crest Trail (see No. 59) and turn left. Climb to the Upper Sandy Guard Station, switchback twice and traverse above the large cabin. Curve right and after 0.2 mile descend to Ramona Falls.

Cross Ramona Creek near the base of the Falls on planks and after several yards come to the beginning of the Yocum Ridge Trail. On the return you can make a scenic loop beside Ramona Creek by following the trail that continues straight (left) here (see No. 50). Keep right and traverse up the wooded slope at a steady grade for three-quarters mile. Switchback right and keep right at the junction of a rerouted section of the Pacific Crest Trail (see No. 59). Traverse the south side of the ridge for 1.2 miles then switchback left. After one-half mile wind up to near the crest of the ridge then resume traversing. At 5.4 miles pass above a scree area and switchback left. Climb a short distance to a large pond and a well-framed scene of Mt. Hood. As attractive as the setting is, a better spot for a snack stop is one-third mile farther beside a stream. Curve around near the north side of the pond and climb moderately to the recommended rest stop at a campsite. Fill your bottles here as this is the last good source of water.

The trail turns left (north) at the campsite — it does not cross the stream — and winds up through attractive woods. Come to a sighting of Mounts St. Helens, Rainier and Adams then switchback and pass a viewpoint featuring Mt. Hood. Cross to the southwest side of the ridge and traverse at a moderate grade along the frequently grassy slopes. Eventually, you will be able to see Paradise Park on the southwestern side of Mt. Hood just above timberline and pinnacle-topped Mt. Jefferson on the horizon to the south. Continue traversing along increasingly open slopes to a viewpoint at the edge of the deep canyon below the ice fall of Reid Glacier. The trail switchbacks left and climbs a grassy slope for 0.6 mile to the viewpoint.

Aerial view lower Yokum Ridge viewpoint

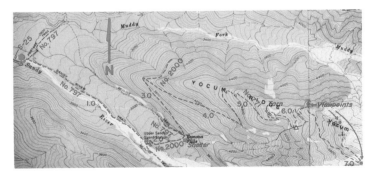

52 DEVILS MEADOW and PARADISE PARK

One day trip or backpack
Distance: 8.5 miles one way
Elevation gain: 2,850 feet; loss 370 feet
High point: 5,790 feet
Allow 5 to 6 hours one way
Usually open mid-July through October
Topographic maps:
   U.S.G.S. Government Camp, Oreg.
   7.5'   1962
   U.S.G.S. Timberline Lodge, Oreg.
   7.5'   1962

Hikers on Zigzag Mountain

If you do this strenuous trip from late August through mid-September be sure to allow extra time for enjoying the fruit of the huckleberry bushes that crowd the trail between 2.5 and 6.0 miles. But regardless of the season, the scenery, the varied terrain and the attractive setting at the destination justify this hike. Since the stone shelter just below Paradise Park is reached by several trails, you can do the hike as a loop or, if you are camping, make side trips north and south along the Timberline Trail (No. 59). By establishing a car shuttle you can return east along the Timberline Trail to Timberline Lodge, the Paradise Park Trail (No. 56) or the Hidden Lake Trail (No. 57).

Proceed on US 26 to the sign on the north side of the highway marking Road 27 located 1.6 miles east of Rhododendron. Turn north, after 0.6 mile curve left, leaving the paved surface, and continue the final four miles to the beginning of Trail No. 779 where the road has been closed. *The last four miles are not passable for vehicles with trailers.*

Walk along the road for two miles to Devils Meadow where a sign to the northeast above the end of the road marks the beginning of the Burnt Lake Trail and lists many mileages. Climb at a gradual grade through woods and more open areas, cross a small stream and 0.5 mile from Devils Meadow come to the junction of the Cast Lake Trail (see No. 48). Keep straight (right), cross a second stream and climb through brush and low trees for a short distance to the junction of the Burnt Lake (No. 49) and Zigzag Mountain Trail. Again keep straight (right), climb steeply, level off then resume climbing and come to the junction of the abandoned Devils Canyon Trail. Keep left and come to a level, open area. Cross the old burn then climb moderately along the slope

of brush and a few scattered trees and at 4.9 miles come to a fine viewpoint where you probably will want to take a long snack stop. Your destination is the meadow across the valley at timberline on the southwest shoulder of Mt. Hood.

Wind down to a narrow ridge, keeping left where a short side path heads off to the right, then hike along the saddle. Begin climbing through deep woods, cross a small stream at 6.8 miles then travel on the level to the junction of the Paradise Park Trail. Turn left and climb for a short distance to the junction of the Pacific Crest Trail No. 2000. This new two mile section was constructed in 1972-73 to enable horse traffic to by-pass fragile Paradise Park. Refer to the appropriate section of No. 59 for a description of the short, scenic loop you can make by heading north from Paradise Park along the Timberline Trail to the junction with No. 2000 then hiking south on the latter to this intersection.

Keep straight and climb through woods and lush grassy clearings for 0.5 mile to the junction with the Timberline Trail and turn left. Walk along the slope of grass, wild flowers and clusters of evergreens for one-quarter mile then traverse into the small canyon formed by Lost Creek. Climb the opposite wall and come to the stone shelter. The open meadows of Paradise Park proper are upslope behind the bluff above the shelter and exploring this expanse is an enjoyable side trip.

Lost Creek

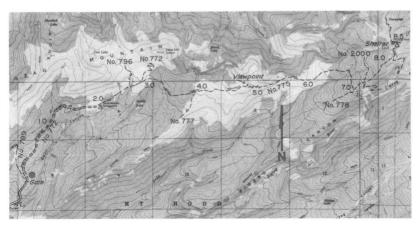

53 FLAG MOUNTAIN

One-half day trip
Distance: 2.1 miles one way
Elevation gain: 790 feet; loss 200 feet
High point: 2,540 feet
Allow 1 to 1½ hours one way
Usually open March through December
Topographic map:
    U.S.G.S. Rhododendron, Oreg.
    7.5'   **1962**

Flag Mountain is a two-mile long, wooded ridge paralleling US 26 just east of Rhododendron. The trail that climbs and descends along its crest affords views of Mt. Hood, Castle Canyon (No. 45) and other landmarks in the immediate area. Rhododendron bushes are plentiful along most of the route so the trip is more attractive during their blooming period from late May to late June. Since the trail ends at a road you could establish a car shuttle and do the hike one way only. Carry water as none is available along the route.

Drive on US 26 to the east end of Rhododendron and turn south on 20 Road, also called Vine Maple Road. After 0.1 mile cross a bridge over the Zigzag River and continue 0.8 mile on 20 Road to a sign marking Road 20E on your left. Turn left and go 100 feet to a sign identifying the beginning of the Flag Mountain Trail. Parking for a few cars is available here. (If you are establishing a car shuttle, first continue east on US 26 to 32 Road which becomes Road 32A, turn south and drive approximately 1.2 miles to a sign on your right stating Flag Mountain Trail.)

Climb above some summer homes at a moderately steep grade for several hundred yards then switchback a few times and come to the crest of the ridge. Continue uphill at a steep angle then at 0.6 mile begin hiking at a gradual grade. During the walk along the gentle summit ridge you will have many views of the southwest side of Mt. Hood. The woods become denser and the trail begins a series of short, alternating drops and rises before the final 0.3 mile descent to Road S32A.

Trail along the summit of Flag Mountain

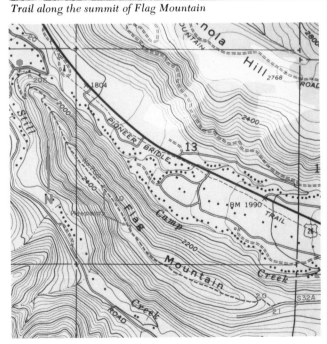

54 DEVILS PEAK

One day trip
Distance: 4.1 miles one way
Elevation gain: 3,205 feet
High point: 5,045 feet
Allow 3 to 3½ hours one way
Usually open late June through mid-November
Topographic maps:
    U.S.G.S. Government Camp, Oreg.
    7.5'   **1962**
    U.S.G.S. Rhododendron, Oreg.
    7.5'   **1962**

In the 1890's forest rangers patrolled the woods on horseback and visited suitable highpoints to scan the surrounding slopes for signs of a fire. Then, in the early 1900's, the Osborne fire finder was developed and permanent vantage points were established. At first, these were just leveled stumps to hold the fire finder. Then tents were erected and later the more familiar towers were built. As early as the 1920's the feasibility of using airplanes in fire fighting was considered and during the 1960's aerial surveillance was used increasingly. Because the lookouts are no longer needed in the Mt. Hood region and their deteriorating condition would be unsightly and dangerous, Forest Service personnel have dismantled or burned most of the towers and ground houses that perched on high points around Mt. Hood.

The climb to Devils Peak visits the one lookout in the Hood area accessible only by trail. (One other hike in this guide, No. 69 to Bull of the Woods in the Clackamas River drainage, visits a standing tower.) Typical of lookout sites, the view is far-ranging and includes Mounts St. Helens, Adams and Rainier to the north, Mt. Hood close by to the northeast and the Salmon River drainage, Salmon Butte, Mt. Jefferson and Three Fingered Jack to the south. Start the hike with a full bottle of water in case the stream at 1.8 miles is not flowing. You can do the trip as a fun, but strenuous, loop by returning on the long ridge that forms Hunchback Mountain (No. 41). The circuit would involve four additional miles, 750 feet of extra climbing and a very short car shuttle.

Drive on US 26 to 10 Road located 0.3 mile west of Rhododendron and turn south. After 0.3 mile keep right and continue on the paved surface for 3.1 miles to a sign on the right (south) side of the road identifying the beginning of the Cool Creek Trail. (10 Road becomes 12 Road.) A few turnouts for parking are situated off the north side of the road near the marker. You also can reach the trailhead by following 20 Road at the east end of Rhododendron for one mile to the junction with 12 Road. Turn left and continue the final 1.8 miles to the trailhead.

Climb at a sometimes steep grade for several hundred feet then begin winding up the slope until reaching the ridge top. Walk along the crest for a short distance then traverse along a north facing slope at a moderate grade. Make a set of very short switchbacks and pass an open spot where you have a good view of Mt. Hood. For the next three-quarters mile follow a course of short switchbacks and traverses then curve into a large, wooded basin. Go in and out of a small side canyon and at a second one cross a small stream. Two-tenths mile farther switchback left and climb along the slope then begin a series of several short switchbacks.

Continue climbing through woods then at 2.9 miles traverse at a gradual grade to a saddle on the narrow ridge crest. Resume climbing and as you gain elevation pass a few rocky, open areas that afford good views to the east then traverse on the west side just below the rim of the ridge's precipitous east face. At 3.9 miles pass a helispot at a saddle and climb steeply for a short distance to a junction. Turn right and traverse through woods for 75 yards to a sign pointing left to Devils Peak Lookout. If you make the loop along Hunchback Ridge you will be following the main trail that curves right here. To reach the summit, turn left, after several yards pass an outhouse on your right and come to the lookout.

Devils Peak Lookout

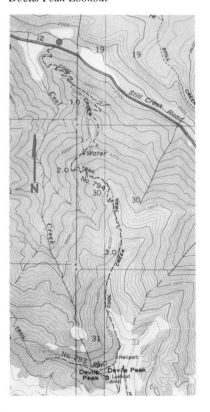

55 PIONEER BRIDLE TRAIL

One day trip
Distance: 4 miles one way
Elevation gain: 1,120 feet
High point: 3,600 feet
Allow 2 to 2½ hours one way
Usually open mid-May through mid-November
Topographic map:
  U.S.G.S. Government Camp, Oreg.
  7.5'   1962

The Pioneer Bridle Trail, that generally parallels US 26 for eight miles east of Rhododendron, was built by Civilian Conservation Corps crews in 1935. The westerly portion of the trail travels on the level between the highway and summer homes but the final four miles described below follows a considerably more interesting route: the trail climbs the southern shoulder of Laurel Hill, passes an abandoned mine shaft, goes through a tunnel built under the old Mt. Hood Highway and follows a portion of the Barlow Road. On your return you can make a short side loop down the western tip of Little Zigzag Canyon. Since the hike ends near US 26, you can do the trip one way only by establishing a car shuttle.

Drive on US 26 four miles east of Rhododendron or five miles west of Government Camp to a large sign identifying the road to Twin Bridges and Barlow Campgrounds. Park your car in the large turnout on the north side of the highway just east of the junction. An old carved wooden sign stating Pioneer Bridle Trail identifies the beginning of the hike. (If you plan to establish a car shuttle first drive on US 26 to a road across the highway from the western end of the Ski Bowl access road, one mile west of Government Camp. Turn north and drive a few hundred yards to a sign identifying the terminus of the Pioneer Bridle Trail.)

A few yards beyond the wooden sign keep right at a fork and walk almost on the level for 0.2 mile through a forest of small trees and rhododendron bushes. Enter deep woods and climb in a few loose switchbacks. Continue uphill, come to an old burn and pass through a grove of alder. Traverse at a moderate grade then enter deeper woods and climb more noticeably to the crest of Laurel Hill. Travel on the level for a short distance then climb in deep woods before traversing a rocky slope. After a glimpse of

Mt. Hood pass an old mine shaft on your left just off the trail. Begin descending gradually and come to an open area where a scree slope on your right extends up to US 26. Re-enter woods and hike beside the remains of an attractive wall then pass through the little tunnel.

To reach a relaxing spot for a snack stop turn left several yards beyond the tunnel and descend along the old highway. Cross the bridge over Little Zigzag Creek, turn right and walk to the shaded, flat area beside the stream. If you make the recommended loop you will be returning along the path that heads upstream here.

To continue the hike climb moderately beyond the tunnel and where you meet an old road keep left. However, do not veer too far left or you will be on a short spur road to a power line. Pass a sign marking the Little Zigzag Canyon Trail, the path you will follow if you make the loop. Continue uphill and where the road forks keep left. The other branch meets the old highway after several hundred feet. Enter deeper woods and cross a small creek. Continue through the woods and jump a second stream. Several yards from the flow curve right and occasionally travel on a planked portion of the old Barlow Road. Keep straight where a road joins on the right and after a short distance come to the end of the hike at the old highway.

To make the side loop, traverse downhill along the Little Zigzag Canyon Trail. Cross a stream on a pole bridge, pass an attractive waterfall and continue descending to the old highway at the snack stop.

Trail sign

56 PARADISE PARK TRAIL

One day trip or backpack
Distance: 5.6 miles one way
Elevation gain: 3,000 feet
High point: 5,800 feet
Allow 3½ to 4 hours one way
Usually open mid-July through October
Topographic maps:
  U.S.G.S. Government Camp, Oreg.
  7.5'   1962
  U.S.G.S. Timberline Lodge, Oreg.
  7.5'   1962

Lost Creek

Paradise Park is an expanse of grassy slopes just above timberline on the southwestern shoulder of Mt. Hood. In August, when the wild flowers are at their prime, the name of the area is especially appropriate. In addition to the Timberline Trail (No. 59) that passes the stone shelter just below the Park, another hike ends at the structure. By establishing a car shuttle you could return along the Timberline Trail to Timberline Lodge or along the second route to Devils Meadow (No. 52). Another shorter loop, that involves three additional miles and 1,000 feet of elevation gain and a 0.9 mile car shuttle or road walk follows the Hidden Lake Trail (No. 57). If you want to return along the same route you followed up but still would like to enjoy some more of the exceptionally scenic area near Paradise Park you could make a two mile loop that heads north from the shelter to the junction with a new section of No. 2000 and follows it south to the intersection with the Paradise Park Trail. The only water available before the destination is from a stream at 3.8 miles.

Proceed on US 26 four miles east of Rhododendron or five miles west of Government Camp to a road on the north side of the highway marked by a sign indicating the route to Twin Bridges and Barlow Campgrounds. Turn north and follow the road for 1.1 miles to the entrance to Twin Bridges Campground and turn left. Cross a bridge, curve right and after 60 yards come to a sign on your left marking the beginning of the Paradise Park Trail. A few parking spaces are available between the trees near the sign.

Walk on the level for a few hundred feet then switchback up to the left. Curve right and climb at a very moderate grade. At 0.5 mile turn left and traverse for another 0.5 mile then curve right and travel through deeper woods. Switchback twice and begin the 3.5 mile climb along the ridge to the west of Zigzag Canyon. Near 2.3 miles come near the edge of a bluff above the Zigzag River. Hike on the crest of a narrow ridge and at 3.2 miles walk through an open area then reenter woods and 0.5 mile beyond the clearing pass a stream, the only source of water before the destination. Continue up through woods of exceptionally large trees and at 4.5 miles come to the junction of the trail from Devils Meadow.

Keep right and climb somewhat more steeply for 0.2 mile to the junction of a new section of the Pacific Crest Trail No. 2000. Keep straight and climb the remaining 0.5 mile through woods and small clearings to the Timberline Trail. Turn left and traverse along the tree-dotted slope of grass and flowers for one-quarter mile. Drop slightly into the small canyon formed by Lost Creek then climb the opposite wall for a few hundred feet to the stone shelter.

To make the short loop, continue north from the shelter for 0.7 mile then descend and come to the junction of No. 2000. Turn left and follow it to the intersection with the Paradise Park Trail. You also could hike east from the shelter along the Timberline Trail to the eastern end of the by-pass and walk west to the Paradise Park Trail. Refer to No. 57 and the appropriate section of No. 59 for a detailed description of this alternate loop and of the route to the Hidden Lake Trail or Timberline Lodge.

Paradise Park shelter

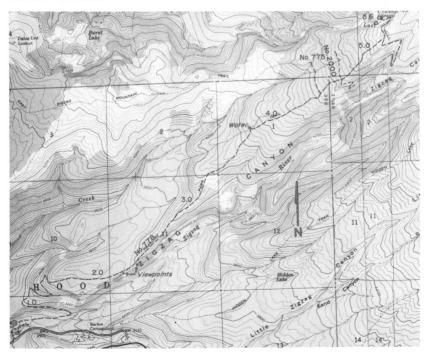

One day trip or backpack
Distance: 5 miles one way
Elevation gain: 2,770 feet
High point: 5,850 feet
Allow 3 to 3½ hours one way
Usually open mid-July through October
Topographic maps:
    U.S.G.S. Government Camp, Oreg.
    7.5'   **1962**
    U.S.G.S. Timberline Lodge, Oreg.
    7.5'   **1962**

The Hidden Lake Trail climbs the length of the wooded ridge separating Zigzag and Little Zigzag Canyons and meets the Timberline Trail at a point one and one-half miles west of Timberline Lodge and three miles east of Paradise Park. You can make a long, strenuous loop by combining this hike with the one along the Paradise Park Trail (No. 56). The middle portion of this circuit follows the scenic Timberline Trail for about 2.5 miles and includes the hike in and out of deep Zigzag Canyon. The loop would add three miles and 1,000 feet of elevation gain and necessitate establishing a short car shuttle or a walk of 0.9 mile along a road. By making a longer shuttle you could return east on the Timberline Trail to Timberline Lodge. The only water source along the Hidden Lake Trail is at 2.2 miles.

Drive on US 26 four miles east of Rhododendron or five miles west of Government Camp to a road on the north side of the highway marked by a sign indicating the route to Twin Bridges and Barlow Campgrounds. Turn north and follow the road for two miles to a large turnout on your left where a sign identifies the beginning of the Hidden Lake Trail.

Immediately begin climbing and soon make several short switchbacks. After affording a glimpse of Mt. Hood the route straightens out and continues climbing at a moderate grade, except for one short steep stretch, along the wooded, increasingly broad crest. Rhododendron bushes are plentiful and during July their pink blossoms add color to the light green hue of the forest. Drop slightly, travel at a gradual grade then make one switchback and cross a small footbridge. A short distance beyond the span come to the junction of the side path to Hidden Lake. To reach it turn right and walk 200 feet to near the west end.

To resume the hike keep left on the main trail and travel uphill for 0.2 mile to an easy stream crossing, the one source of water along the climb. The trail switchbacks after about 0.1 mile and continues up the wooded crest. Near 3.8 miles pass close to the rim of Zigzag Canyon then climb more noticeably and traverse the southeastern slope of a little side canyon before meeting the Timberline Trail.

If you are returning along the Paradise Park Trail turn left and after 0.8 mile wind down into Zigzag Canyon. Traverse up the western wall and where you come to the first switchback keep straight (left) on No. 2000. After 0.5 mile meet the junction of the Paradise Park Trail and turn left. While making this loop you could visit Paradise Park with little additional mileage or elevation gain. (See the appropriate section of No. 59 for a detailed description of the route.)

Waterfall above the crossing of the Zigzag River

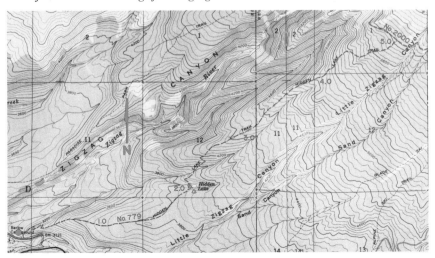

58 ALPINE TRAIL

One day trip
Distance: 3 miles one way
Elevation gain: 1,980 feet
High point: 5,940 feet
Allow 3 hours one way
Usually open July through October
Topographic map:
U.S.G.S. Timberline Lodge, Oreg.
7.5'   1962

Lower Alpine Trail

Skiers who have negotiated the Alpine Ski Trail between Timberline Lodge and Government Camp during winter especially will enjoy covering the same terrain on foot. While climbing along this trail you will have frequent views of the south side of Mt. Hood and on the return you can look across to the Multorpor-Ski Bowl Ski Areas and down to Trillium Lake. Wild strawberries thrive on the open slopes of Summit Ski Area during July and while searching for the succulent little fruit you also can be watching for change, combs, ski pole baskets and other debris from hapless skiers. With good reason, Forest Service personnel refer to this trail as the "Silver Find." If you locate enough money you can pay for refreshments at Timberline Lodge and consume them while enjoying the view from one of the building's balconies. Also, you may want to visit the two main lobbies and examine the fine craftsmanship of the wood, metal and stone work. Carry water as none is available until the end of the hike.

Proceed on US 26 to Government Camp and leave your car in the large parking area for the Summit Ski Area at the east end of town just before the Business Loop rejoins the main highway. Restrooms are located at the east end of the parking area.

Walk up the dirt road between the Ski Patrol Cabin and the Day Lodge. Climb along the open slope, paralleling the east side of the tow, then curve right and continue rising to the top end of the upper tow. Hike along a two track road that eventually narrows onto a trail and near 0.9 mile briefly come close to the West Leg Road, the first route up to the area now occupied by Timberline Lodge. It was replaced in the late 1940's by the present, paved road to the east. The numbers nailed on the trees at regular intervals mark the route and help skiers give their exact location if help is needed.

The grade increases considerably as the trail climbs Big Mazama Hill then becomes more moderate beyond the crest. Purple lupine and the creamy white petals of the Mariposa lily are two of the wild flowers found along the route. If you turn around you can look across the valley to the Multopor and Ski Bowl Ski Areas. The name for the most easterly of the two was taken from the butte that was named after the Multopor Republican Club of Portland whose members created the word by combining the first letters of Multnomah, Oregon and Portland.

Pass the junction of the Glade Ski Trail on your left at 2.5 miles and continue up the wide swath. The cement foundation blocks you pass are the last remnants of a tramway that operated for a few years around the early 1950's and the route of the two gondolas, that resemble giant streetcars, followed part of the Glade Trail. Curve right along a road, walk under a lift and come to Timberline Lodge. The Lodge was a Works Progress Administration project and was constructed in the incredibly short time of 21 months in the mid 1930's. Construction of a new, east wing was started in 1972.

Front door of Timberline Lodge

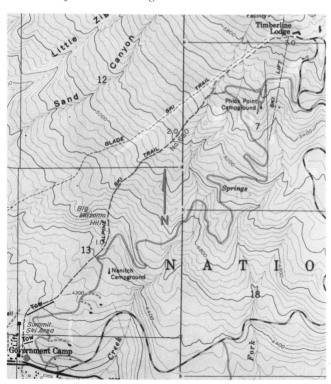

59 TIMBERLINE TRAIL

Backpack
Distance: 37.6 miles round trip (40 miles round trip including Elk Meadows)
Elevation gain: 9,800 feet; loss 9,800 feet
High point: 7,350 feet
Allow 3 to 5 days round trip
Usually open mid-July through mid-October
Topographic maps:
   U.S.G.S. Badger Lake, Oreg.
   7.5'   1962
   U.S.G.S. Bull Run Lake, Oreg.
   7.5'   1962
   U.S.G.S. Cathedral Ridge, Oreg.
   7.5'   1962
   U.S.G.S. Government Camp, Oreg.
   7.5'   1962
   U.S.G.S. Timberline Lodge, Oreg.
   7.5'   1962

In 1892 Will Langille, an early climbing guide on the north side of Mt. Hood, and a companion made the first circuit around the peak on foot. Forty-two years later Civilian Conservation Corps crews began constructing a trail around the mountain. The work was completed in September of 1938 and since then hikers and backpackers have followed the Timberline Trail through some of the most scenic terrain in Oregon. Although the route generally circles the mountain near timberline, it occasionally drops into deeper woods or climbs above the zone of any vegetation. Along almost all sections of the Timberline Trail the impressive, glaciated faces of Mt. Hood dominate the view.

Although most of the many varieties of wild flowers along the trail generally bloom during the first part of August, the circuit always is exceptionally scenic. Through July fording the streams fed by glacier melt — particularly Eliot Creek and the White River — may present some problems. If the snowfall on the mountain has been exceptionally heavy, the date the route is open may be delayed. Although water is plentiful along most sections of the Timberline Trail, it is a good idea always to keep your bottle at least half full. Use only water from side creeks as glacier fed streams contain rock flour that may irritate the lining of your intestinal tract.

Most backpackers start at Timberline Lodge and hike in a clockwise direction but you can begin the loop at any of the many entry points and travel either direction. Near 13.4 and 25.2 miles the Timberline Trail passes close to roads (see No's. 27 and 34) but the remaining accesses are along side trails. These many side routes make it possible to do the Timberline Trail in sections if you do not have the time or inclination for a long backpack.

A few hardy joggers have run around Mt. Hood without a layover — a circuit that takes about 9 to 12 hours. Of course, most people choose to carry camping equipment and adopt a more leisurely pace. The usual time for a complete circuit with few, if any, side trips is three or four days. However, if you have the time, many extremely scenic and interesting side excursions are possible and allowing four nights and five days would provide ample time for investigating most of the features off the main trail.

Drive on US 26 one-half mile east of Government Camp or two and one-half miles west of the junction of Oregon 35 and US 26 to the road to Timberline Lodge. Turn north and proceed 5½ miles to the large parking area below the Lodge.

Timberline Lodge to Paradise Park
Distance: 4.7 miles
Elevation gain: 1,100 feet; loss 1,380 feet

Walk to the west end of the Lodge, turn right and go uphill for 100 yards to a huge, carved wooden sign that marks the start of the Timberline Trail and lists mileages to many places along the route. For the next 13.4 miles and along the final 1.5 miles of the loop you simultaneously will be following the Timberline and Pacific Crest Trails. Turn left and traverse near timberline at a gradual downhill grade. Pinnacle-topped Mt. Jefferson is the high point on the southern horizon. After three-quarters mile watching for a foundation and fallen chimney 75 feet below the trail. They are all that remains of the Timberline Cabin, built in 1915 and used by skiers and climbers until the early 1950's. A short distance farther traverse in and out of Sand Canyon then just beyond it cross Little Zigzag Canyon. At 1.2 miles keep straight (right) at the junction of the Hidden Lake Trail (No. 57) and begin winding down through deeper woods for a few tenths mile then traverse open, grassy slopes. At 2.0 miles, where you travel below the crest of a low sandy ridge, leave the trail and climb several yards for an impressive view down into Zigzag Canyon and up to the rock mass of Mississippi Head at the beginning of the canyon. The unusual

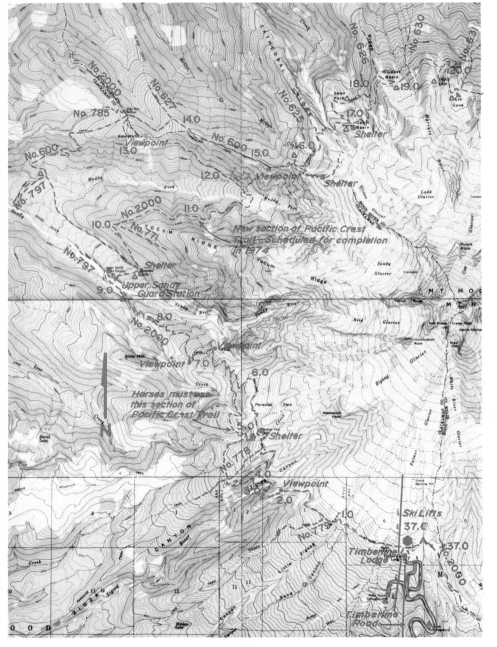

name for this landmark originated in 1905 when the Mississippi delegation to the National Editorial Association conference being held in Portland asked to have Mt. Hood illuminated with fireworks. This site was chosen and named for the group.

Begin descending and switchback down to the floor of the canyon, an elevation loss of 800 feet. Ford the Zigzag River and traverse up the opposite wall. Two-tenths mile from the crossing at the first switchback come to the junction of a new section of the Pacific Crest Trail, built during 1972-73 to enable horse traffic to by-pass the fragile vegetation of Paradise Park. Although this new portion traverses attractive terrain, the best route is along the Timberline Trail. However, if you are spending the first night at Paradise Park, you can make a small loop along the new section of No. 2000 and not miss any scenery.

To reach Paradise Park turn right at the junction and continue climbing along the wooded wall. Switchback once up a sandy, treeless area then traverse along the brush covered slopes of a side canyon. Hike along more gentle, grassy terrain and pass the junction of the trail from Devils Meadow (No. 52) and Twin Bridges Campground (No. 56). The route from Twin Bridges to Paradise Park was built by Forest Service crews in 1923 with funds donated by Simon Benson, builder of the Benson Hotel in Portland. Keep straight (right) and after one-quarter mile come to the little canyon formed by Lost Creek. Traverse down to the stream then climb the opposite wall and come to the stone shelter below Paradise Park, the first good choice for a campsite. The meadows of Paradise Park proper are above timberline to the east and north of the shelter.

If you have the time and desire to make the three mile loop along the by-pass, continue north from the shelter along the Timberline Trail for 0.7 mile then descend and come to the junction of the alternate route. Turn left and follow it to the junction with No. 778. Turn left again and climb for 0.5 mile through lush clearings and woods to the junction of the Timberline Trail.

If you are by-passing Paradise Park, keep left at 3.4 miles. Traverse then make two sets of switchbacks and come to a viewpoint above a slide. Curve right, meet the junction of No. 778 and continue straight. Traverse at a gradual grade in and out of small side canyons with streams and little waterfalls. At the last and largest canyon you will have views of Mt. St. Helens as well as Mt. Hood. Enter deeper woods and descend slightly then cross two small streams and come to the junction of the Timberline Trail.

Paradise Park to Ramona Falls
Distance: 4.8 miles
Elevation gain: 350 feet; loss 2,600 feet

Continue north from the shelter at Paradise Park and walk along the base of a high rock bluff. Go through a sandy little canyon then continue along a gentle, treeless slope. If you want to make a short side trip to Hardesty Rock look right (east) just beyond the sandy stretch for a large, dark, fractured boulder about 200 yards off the trail. Pass a weathered sign pointing to Slide Mountain on the main route then begin descending and soon come to timberline. At 6.3 miles meet the junction of the bypass trail below Paradise Park. Keep right and continue winding downhill. Come to a sign marking the Reid Glacier Viewpoint that also affords a good look at the south side of Yocum Ridge. Keep descending and pass another sign pointing west to Slide Mountain. A short distance farther the route enters deeper woods and continues dropping in loose switchbacks.

At 8.8 miles pass a path on your left to a large, shaded campsite beside Rushing Water Creek. (The areas near the shelters at Paradise Park and Ramona Falls, the spot at the low crossing of the Muddy Fork and this site are the most satisfactory camping places between Timberline Lodge and Cairn Basin at 17.0 miles.) A few hundred feet beyond the campsite leave the deep woods and come to the broad high water stream bed of the Sandy River. Ford a creek and a few yards farther cross the main flow. Follow the obvious path along the sandy stream bed for one-quarter mile then climb the northern bank and come to the junction of No. 797, the southern half of the Ramona Falls Loop (No. 50). Turn right and climb to the Upper Sandy Guard Station. Curve right then switchback left and traverse above the stone structure. The trail travels at a gradual grade for 0.2 mile to the wooden shelter just before lovely Ramona Falls.

Ramona Falls to Cairn Basin
Distance: 7.3 miles
Elevation gain: 2,300 feet; loss 350 feet

Cross Ramona Creek near the base of the Falls and after several yards come to the

Crossing Ladd Creek (above) Mt. Hood from the west (below)

junction of another new section of No. 2000. You can follow this higher route or keep straight on the Timberline Trail. If you decide to take the low route keep straight (left) and descend through attractive woods beside Ramona Creek, crossing the stream twice on little footbridges. Two miles from the Falls come to the junction of No. 797 (see No. 50), keep straight (right) and pass a good campsite. Cross the Muddy Fork on a small bridge and begin winding up the northern wall of the valley. At the rim begin traveling at a more moderate grade and after 0.6 mile come to the junction of the new section of No. 2000 at the former site of the Bald Mountain shelter.

If you choose to follow the new route keep right at the junction just beyond Ramona Falls and traverse up the wooded slope at a steady grade for three-quarters mile. Switchback right and come to the junction of the outstandingly scenic trail along Yocum Ridge (No. 51). This section beyond Ramona Falls and the trail that continues along the south side of the ridge was the original route of the Timberline Trail. It was to have climbed above timberline on Yocum Ridge then traversed north along the base of the Sandy Glacier. However, construction of the trail stopped 1.8 miles beyond Ramona Falls when the engineers decided it was not feasible to build and maintain a trail across slopes that would be snow covered most of the summer.

Keep left at the junction of No. 771 and traverse the northern slope of Yocum Ridge for 1.6 miles to the ford of the Muddy Fork. Walk through a brushy area near the stream bed, drop slightly then begin climbing in woods. One mile from the crossing the trail traverses the open slope below the summit of Bald Mountain. Curve right and 100 yards before the junction of No. 600 pass a path, that may be unmarked, on your right to the summit of Bald Mountain (No. 27). A large, level area at the site of the former Bald Mountain shelter is a good spot to pitch a tent but the nearest water is one-quarter mile away down the Top Spur Trail No. 785 (see No. 27).

Follow east on the Timberline Trail as indicated by the sign pointing to Cairn Basin and Eden Park and descend slightly then begin climbing moderately. One-half mile from the four-way junction keep right at the sign marking the McGee Creek Trail No. 627. When the Timberline Trail was com-

pleted the portion of the Bull Run Reserve where entry was prohibited extended considerably farther east than the present boundary and trails to the west from the Timberline Trail, such as the McGee Creek and Cathedral Ridge Trails and the route along the Sandy River, were closed to public travel. The route climbs more noticeably to a narrow wooded crest then continues uphill and crosses a treeless portion of Bald Mountain Ridge. As you traverse the grassy slope you will have good views of the west face of Mt. Hood, down into the rugged canyon at the head of the Sandy River and the north side of Yocum Ridge. Descend for a short distance into timber then begin winding uphill. Where the trail turns sharply right at 15.7 miles a short spur leads to a campsite. Soon traverse at a more moderate grade and hop a small stream a short distance before crossing the mossy stones of shallow McGee Creek. Make a few short switchbacks then walk through a grassy area beside a large tarn. The trail climbs above another tarn, goes over the crest of a low ridge and comes to the junction of the Cathedral Ridge Trail (No. 28) above some more tarns. The large body of water visible to the northwest is Lost Lake. Curve right and traverse in and out of a small swale.

If you want to make a side trip to the stone shelter on McNeil Point to the south, turn right at the center of the grassy swale and climb cross-country along the floor of the little valley for several hundred yards then rise more steeply for about 200 feet and intersect an obvious path, a section of the original, higher route of the Timberline Trail that was not completed. Turn right and traverse to the south. Where the path is faint along one short stretch veer slightly left and look ahead to where the route crosses a rocky slope. Continue traversing and one-quarter mile from where you intersected the path above the swale come to a crest. Bear slightly right and descend gradually for the final few hundred yards to the stone shelter. A use path winds very steeply down from the structure and intersects the Timberline Trail at 15.7 miles. Ironically, the man for whom the point and subsequently the shelter were named, journalist and author Fred McNeil, preferred wooden shelters as he thought they blended more satisfactorily with the surroundings and that stone ones too closely resembled prison cells.

Near crossing of the Muddy Fork (above) McNeil shelter (below)

To continue the trek along the Timberline Trail climb a short distance from the swale and come to a crest identified by a sign as Cathedral Ridge. Keep left at a fork just beyond the marker and descend to the ford of the South Fork of Ladd Creek. The trail climbs a short distance, crosses a little plateau of grass and scattered trees then descends in one switchback to a junction at Cairn Basin. Good campsites are available near the stone shelter 100 feet to the right (east).

Cairn Basin to Cloud Cap
Distance: 8.4 miles
Elevation gain: 1,800 feet; loss 1,350 feet

The trail to the left (west) at the junction just west of the Cairn Basin shelter is the lower route of the Timberline Trail through Eden Park to Wy'east Basin. If you want to follow this route continue downhill along the open slope with a few short switchbacks. Enter woods, curve right and pass through Eden Park to the ford of Ladd Creek. Climb through woods and a few small open areas to the junction of the Vista Ridge Trail (No. 29). Turn right and traverse gradually uphill for 0.2 mile to Wy'east Basin and the junction of the high section of the Timberline Trail.

If you intend to follow the slightly shorter, higher new section of No. 600 continue along the trail that passes the north side of the shelter at Cairn Basin and drop slightly to the ford of Ladd Creek. Climb along a timbered slope and pass through a clearing then resume traveling up through woods. The route crosses over a low ridge and traverses downhill along an open slope to the junction with the other stretch of the Timberline Trail at Wy'east Basin. An exceptionally scenic side trip from here is the cross-country climb of Barrett Spur (No. 29). Geologists think this massive rock outcropping is the remnant of a volcanic peak that existed before the formation of Mt. Hood.

Traverse to the northeast along the Timberline Trail at a gradual uphill grade and 0.1 mile from Wy'east Basin come to the junction of the Pinnacle Ridge Trail No. 630 that may not be marked. Keep right and after 0.4 mile pass the short side path to Dollar Lake on your right. If you make the trip to this circular tarn continue uphill beyond the lake to the south for a few hundred yards to a viewpoint above Elk Cove. The main route goes over "99" Ridge and traverses

down to Elk Cove, a good choice for a campsite. Cross a creek and pass several yards west of the remains of a stone shelter that was destroyed by an avalanche. Near the north edge of the Cove keep right at the junction of the Elk Cove Trail No. 631 (No. 30).

Wind down gradually through woods for 0.6 mile to the plank bridge across Coe Creek. Be careful on the opposite bank as the rocks may be slippery. Negotiating the original crossing, 0.5 mile upstream, was considerably more demanding: steel cables were installed to aid in the descent and climb of the steep banks and rockfall usually accompanied the hiker on his way down and up. The new route climbs out of Coe Creek canyon in a series of irregular switchbacks then traverses at a gradual grade near timberline. Cross Compass Creek and eventually begin climbing along the wooded western slope of Stranahan Ridge. Go over the crest and descend in and out of small side canyon to the ford of Eliot Creek. One-quarter mile farther come to the junction of No. 600A and the campground at Cloud Cap saddle.

To visit Cloud Cap Inn turn left and walk 75 feet through the campground to Road S12. Cross the road and locate a path that heads north up the crest for 200 yards to the old hotel that opened in the late 1880's. Although now closed to the public, the building is maintained by the Hood River Crag Rats, a climbing club. Cloud Cap Inn was not the first resort here: in 1883 David Cooper, an early settler in the Hood River Valley, and two other men built the first road to Cloud Cap. The following year Cooper pitched a cook tent and several sleeping tents in a draw below the site of the present Inn and he acted as climbing guide, his wife operated the resort and Oscar Stranahan, one of the partners in the road, drove the stage.

Cloud Cap to Elk Meadows
Distance: 5.6 miles
Elevation gain: 1,650 feet; loss 2,300 feet

Be sure to fill your bottles at Cloud Cap as the water sources are not dependable for the next four miles. Although you can follow No. 600A through Tilly Jane Campground and rejoin the Timberline Trail at 26.2 miles (see No. 32), the main route is more scenic and direct. Continue south on the Timberline Trail and after a couple hundred yards

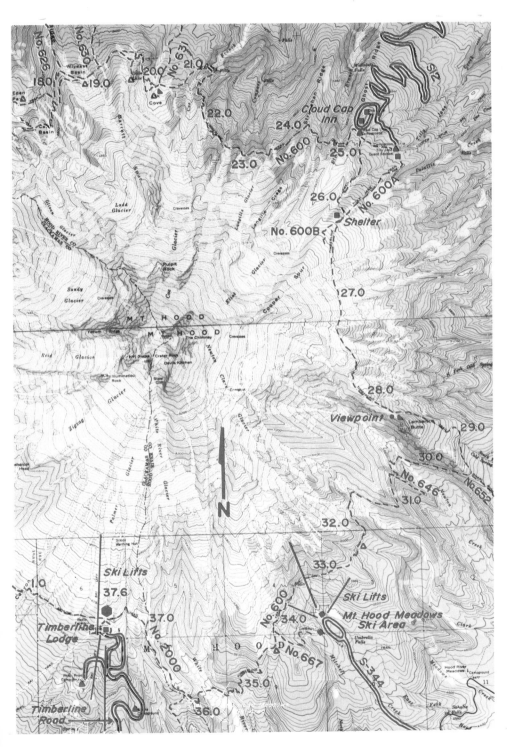

keep left on the main route at the junction of the side path to Eliot Glacier. Hike through woods of thick-trunked conifers then come to a moraine at timberline and climb along the slope of sand and boulders. The trail traverses the wall of a small rocky canyon then curves left and climbs through a swath of stunted pines. Leave the vegetation and traverse a slope of rocks and scattered clumps of grass and other low growing plants. One mile from Cloud Cap come to the junction of the trail from Tilly Jane Campground on your left and the route up Cooper Spur (No. 34) on your right. From this junction you can look north to Mounts St. Helens, Adams and Rainier and the Upper and Lower Hood River Valleys.

Keep straight and continue above timberline, traversing in and out of side canyons. At 27.4 miles come to the highest point along the Timberline Trail. Begin generally descending through more complex terrain then at 28.3 miles come to a sand blasted wooden sign identifying Gnarl Ridge. This impressive viewpoint across from Newton Clark Glacier makes a good rest stop. The route continues gradually downhill along the northern side of Lamberson Butte, passing the ruins of an old stone shelter upslope from the trail, then curves right and begins winding through deeper woods. Traverse for a short distance, pass through a few small open grassy areas and come to the junction of the trail to Elk Meadows. Although reaching Elk Meadows, the largest on Mt. Hood, involves an extra 1.2 miles and 670 feet of elevation loss, the camp sites there are especially attractive. If you plan to visit or camp at the Meadows refer to Trail No's. 35, 36 and 37 for more detailed descriptions of the area.

Elk Meadows to Timberline Lodge
Distance: 9.2 miles
Elevation gain: 2,600 feet; loss 1,820 feet

To complete the loop, traverse gradually downhill to the west along the Timberline Trail from the junction of the route to Elk Meadows at 29.5 miles. Go through a rocky area and cross Newton Creek on a bridge. The route climbs a sparsely wooded slope, curves right and follows the crest of a small ridge that forms the northern side of a little inner valley. Cross the head of the valley and climb along the treeless southern wall. Enter woods and curve right around a considerably larger ridge. Keep right at the junction of the Newton Creek Trail and continue traversing downhill along a large, open sandy slope to the bridge over Clark Creek. After the crossing the route heads upstream a short distance then turns left and begins winding uphill. Cross three streams and continue climbing then round the crest of another ridge. Traverse with brief ups and downs along the slope of large trees and lush, grassy clearings, passing a campsite below the trail at 32.5 miles.

At 33.4 miles come to the Mt. Hood Meadows Ski Area and pass under several chair lifts. Cross some small streams and come to the junction of Trail No. 667 to Umbrella Falls and Hood River Meadows. Keep right and go through a grassy area before entering woods and beginning the winding descent to the broad canyon formed by the White River. Follow stakes across the rocky, sandy bed to a point upstream from the confluence of the two branches. Walk along the bank until you find a suitable place to ford. The established route heads upstream along a bluff then curves left at the edge of the timber. (If you have difficulty locating the trail after the ford, aim for the north end of the woods.) Climb for one-quarter mile to the junction with the Pacific Crest Trail (see No. 63).

Turn right and continue up the open slope of stumps, grass and scattered trees. About 200 yards from the junction the tread stops but tall stakes imbedded in the sandy soil indicate the correct route. The obvious tread soon resumes and the trail follows the crest of the narrow ridge above White River canyon. Begin traversing more gradually uphill along a slope of volcanic ash, go in and out of a small side canyon and walk above Timberline Lodge to the large, carved wooden sign where you began the loop.

Shelter on Cooper Spur Trail (above), waterfall on Clark Creek (lower left), Newton Creek bridge (lower right)

60 MIRROR LAKE and TOM DICK MOUNTAIN

One day trip or backpack
Distance: 3.3 miles one way
Elevation gain: 1,645 feet
High point: 5,066 feet
Allow 2½ hours one way
Usually open late June through mid-November
Topographic map:
   U.S.G.S. Government Camp, Oreg.
   7.5'   1962

Near summit of Tom Dick Mountain

Because of its accessibility and shortness, the 1.2 mile trip to Mirror Lake is the most popular in the Mt. Hood area. Even in the middle of winter the snow along the route usually is tromped down sufficiently to make an easily followed path to the lake. Many spots along the shore afford a good place to enjoy a snack and the view of Mt. Hood. The main trail continues 2.2 miles farther along treeless slopes of huckleberry bushes to the rim of the large bowl that holds Mirror Lake. Leave home with a full bottle of water — do not fill it from the creek at the trailhead as the flow may be contaminated.

Drive on US 26 to a large turnout along the south shoulder of the highway eight miles east of Rhododendron and one mile west of Government Camp. A sign at the footbridge identifies the Mirror Lake Trail.

Cross the narrow, railed bridge over Camp Creek, turn right and after several yards curve left into a small side canyon. Traverse up through deep woods for a short distance to a little footbridge over the outlet creek from Mirror Lake. Wind up through timber for one-third mile to an open area. Switchback left at its western side and recross the

rocky slope. Resume climbing through woods then make the first of several switchbacks. Come to a fork in the trail, keep left, cross a footbridge over the outlet creek and after a few hundred feet come to the northeastern end of Mirror Lake. The path around the lake traverses the rocky slope along the eastern shore then travels through an area of small trees before reaching the large, swampy meadow at the western end.

To continue the hike to the summit of Tom Dick Mountain keep right at the fork just before the lake or intersect the trail from the large meadow. Make a mile long traverse up an open, north-facing slope where huckleberries are plentiful from late August to mid-September. Come to a huge cairn at the crest, turn sharply left and follow the trail along the ridge top. Where the tread becomes faint bear left and go cross-country for a short distance to the rocky summit, the former site of a lookout cabin.

Mirror Lake in February

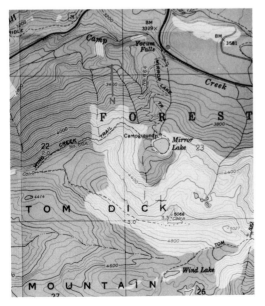

61 VEDA LAKE

One-half day trip
Distance: 1.2 miles one way
Elevation gain: 180 feet; loss 470 feet
High point: 4,690 feet
Allow 30 minutes one way
Usually open late June through October
Topographic maps:
  U.S.G.S. Government Camp, Oreg.
  7.5'   1962
  U.S.G.S. High Rock, Oreg.
  15'   1956

Indian Paintbrush

In 1917 two men packed some trout fry to a small lake south of Mt. Hood and a local forester named it for them by combining the initial two letters of their first names, Vern and Dave. Today, the shore of Veda Lake often is lined with fishermen hoping to catch some progeny of those fry. The circular lake lies in a small, steep-sided bowl and the short climb and descent to it makes an ideal hike for families with children. During late August sampling the tempting fruit on the huckleberry bushes beside the trail may slow progress considerably. Start the hike with an adequate supply of water as none is available along the route.

The seven mile long Fir Tree Loop (No. 62) starts several yards from the beginning of the trail to Veda Lake and you could combine the two if you wanted a more strenuous, longer day of hiking.

Drive on US 26 to the road to Still Creek Campground on the south side of the highway one mile east of Government Camp and two miles west of the junction of US 26 and Oregon 35. Turn south, go downhill and after 0.7 mile keep right on S32C. Four-tenths mile farther turn right on S32 and after another 0.4 mile keep straight on S32, following the sign to Huckleberry Area and Kinzel Lake Campground, then continue the remaining 3.6 miles to a marker for Fir Tree Forest Camp. A sign on the right (north) side of the road identifies the trailhead. Parking space is available in the area south of the road.

Climb at a moderate grade for a short distance then wind up the slope for one-third mile. Traverse along the face of the ridge through deep woods then begin descending and at 0.7 mile come to a viewpoint 400 feet above Veda Lake that also affords a view across to Mt. Hood and Government Camp. This name was given to the site after wagons and other supplies were abandoned there in the fall of 1849 by members of the First U.S. Mounted Rifles. The group had crossed the Plains to The Dalles where most of the men were ferried down the Columbia River to Fort Vancouver. The few remaining soldiers were ordered to take the stock and loaded wagons over the Barlow Road to Oregon City before the animals had recuperated fully. Nearly two-thirds of the animals died on the journey.

Switchback left at the viewpoint and wind down the generally open slope that affords more views of the lake. The grade becomes gradual then travels north above the shoreline. A trail, that becomes a use-path along the southern shore, circles the lake.

Veda Lake

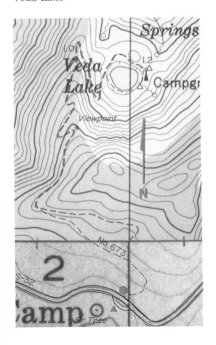

62 FIR TREE LOOP

One day trip
Distance: 7 miles round trip
Elevation gain: 1,650 feet; loss 1,650 feet
(round trip)
High point: 4,450 feet
Allow 3 to 3½ hours round trip
Usually open mid-June through October
Topographic map:
  U.S.G.S. High Rock, Oreg.
    15'   1956

Unlike most hikes, the climbing on this trip is done at the end instead of the beginning. The loop follows three routes, the Fir Tree, Salmon River and Dry Lakes Trails, and although much of the circuit is through woods, in the more open areas wild flowers, including lupine, rhododendron and the infrequent Washington lily, bloom during early summer. The three small stream crossings present no problems.

The 1.2 mile long trail to Veda Lake (No. 61) starts across the road from the beginning of the Fir Tree Loop so you could make the short climb and descent as a warm-up to the longer trip.

Proceed on US 26 to the road to Still Creek Campground on the south side of the highway one mile east of Government Camp and two miles west of the junction of US 26 and Oregon 35. Turn south, go down-hill and after 0.7 mile keep right on S32C. Four-tenths mile farther turn right on S32 and after another 0.4 mile keep straight on S32, following the sign to Huckleberry Area and Kinzel Lake Campground, then continue the remaining 3.6 miles to a marker for Fir Tree Forest Camp. Parking space is available off the south side of the road. A sign on the left (south) shoulder about 100 feet west of the Veda Lake trailhead marks the beginning of the Fir Tree Loop.

For the first few hundred feet blue paint has been sprayed on tree trunks to identify the route as it drops through the campground. The trail becomes obvious and continues down through woods. Eventually begin descending at a more gradual grade and at 0.9 mile make an easy ford of an unnamed stream. The terrain becomes more open and High Rock and Wolf Peak can be seen to the southwest. At 1.2 miles come to the junction of the Dry Lake Trail. You will be returning up this route.

Keep straight and soon begin winding down through denser, more lush vegetation. Just beyond 2.0 miles traverse above a stream you can hear but not see. Curve sharply left and descend for a few tenths mile more through deep woods to the junction of the Salmon River Trail at 3.0 miles. Turn left and walk generally on the level with a few very slight ups and downs. Cross a small scree area and 0.8 mile from the junction cross the stream you forded earlier. Since fresh water is available here and the stream is about midway along the loop, this is a good choice for a snack stop. Continue hiking at a gradual grade then begin climbing and at 4.0 mile switchback to the left. Traverse uphill at a steady, moderate grade then level off and come to the junction of the Dry Lake Trail. The Salmon River Trail continues another 1.5 miles before ending at a logging spur road.

Turn left and climb at an irregular grade, descending briefly at one point. One-half mile from the Salmon River Trail cross the unnamed stream for the third time and after another 0.5 mile of uphill come to the junction of the Fir Tree Trail you were on earlier. Turn right and retrace your steps to the beginning of the hike.

Large blaze along trail

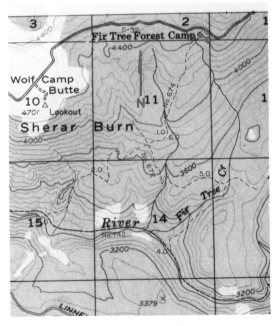

63 PACIFIC CREST TRAIL to TIMBERLINE LODGE

One day trip
Distance: 5.7 miles one way
Elevation gain: 1,890 feet; loss 100 feet
High point: 6,040 feet
Allow 3½ to 4 hours one way
Usually open July through mid-October
Topographic map:
   U.S.G.S. Timberline Lodge, Oreg.
   7.5'   1962

The segment of the Pacific Crest Trail extends from the Canadian to the Mexican border and in Oregon runs from near Cascade Locks on the Columbia River for more than 400 miles south along the backbone of the Cascade Range to the California border southwest of Klamath Falls. The northernmost section of the Trail from the Columbia River to Twin Lakes, located south of Mt. Hood, is covered by seven hikes in this guide — No's. 13, 21, 23, 27, 59, 63 and 64.

The segment of the Pacific Crest Trail from Barlow Pass up to Timberline Lodge rises through deep woods to its junction with the Timberline Trail. The route then climbs above the tree line, following the western rim of broad, rocky White River Canyon, before curving west to the Lodge. In addition to the view of this deep Canyon, the southeast face of Mt. Hood fills the scene to the north. Since both ends of the hike can be reached by road, you can do the trip one way only.

Proceed on Oregon 35 to a small sign identifying the Barlow Road located 2.2 miles east of the junction of US 26 and Oregon 35 and approximately 37.8 miles south of Hood River. Turn south and after 0.2 mile come to a large parking area.

Walk back along the road to the highway or cross the road to a cluster of signs and follow Trail No. 2000 that heads north and is identified by the sign pointing to the Timberline Trail. At the highway turn right and walk 150 feet in an easterly direction to a sign on the north shoulder marking the resumption of the Pacific Crest Trail. Climb along the slope for several yards, enter woods and wind up through the forest for a short distance to an old road. Cross it and traverse through a small logged area. At the face of the ridge you will be looking north toward Mt. Hood and you can turn to the southwest for views of Bird Butte,

Eureka Peak, a portion of the Multorpor Ski Area and East Zigzag Mountain in the distance to the west. Curve along the slope then reenter woods and begin traversing at a gentle grade. Curve gradually left, cross the crest of a low ridge and continue traversing. Pass above a little meadow at 3.0 miles and cross another low ridge. Curve right and traverse below the crest then climb through woods of widely spaced conifers to a clearing. Follow the path through the open area for several hundred feet and come to the junction of the Timberline Trail. From here the Pacific Crest and Timberline Trails follow the same route until Ramona Falls, 11 miles distant on Mt. Hood's west side.

Keep left and continue up the open slope of stumps, grass and scattered trees. About 200 yards from the junction the tread stops but tall stakes imbedded in the sandy soil indicate the correct route. The obvious trail soon resumes and the route follows the crest of the narrow ridge above White River Canyon. If you look closely at the east wall of the canyon below to your right you can see the bleached trunks that comprise the White River Canyon Buried Forest. Geologists think these remains are about 500 years old and were the result of the latest extensive advance of the White River Glacier. At 5.0 miles begin traversing gradually uphill along a slope of volcanic ash, go in and out of a small side canyon and walk above Timberline Lodge. Where you come to a large carved wooden sign listing many mileages turn left and follow the path to the Lodge.

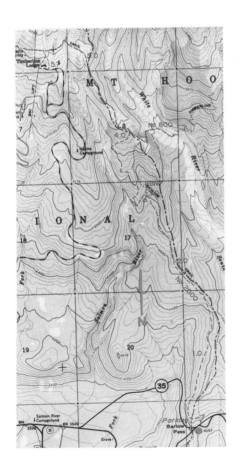

Sign below trail head

64 TWIN LAKES

One day trip or backpack
Distance: 4 miles one way
Elevation gain: 425 feet; loss 200 feet
High point: 4,500 feet
Allow 2½ to 3 hours one way
Usually open late June through mid-November
Topographic maps:
    U.S.G.S. Mt. Wilson, Oreg.
    15'   **1956**
    U.S.G.S. Timberline Lodge, Oreg.
    7.5'   **1962**

Although you will have an entirely pleasing hike just by visiting shallow Upper Twin Lake and its considerably deeper and larger counterpart, you can make an even more enjoyable trip by taking a different route for a portion of the return. This loop, that would add no mileage and 480 feet of elevation gain, goes through a large meadow with a beaver pond and passes a short spur to Palmateer Point that affords views of the broad valley formed by Barlow Creek and across to Mt. Hood and Barlow Butte. Carry water as none is available from streams along the hike.

Proceed on Oregon 35 to a small sign identifying the Barlow Road located 2.2 miles east of the junction of US 26 and Oregon 35 and approximately 37.8 miles south of Hood River. Turn south and after 0.2 mile come to a large parking area. Signs in the woods on the south side of the pavement identify the route of the Pacific Crest and Barlow Butte Trails.

Head southwest (right) and walk up through woods at a gradual grade. During winter and spring this trail is a popular cross-country ski route. Begin climbing more noticeably after 0.5 mile then travel along an open slope, dropping slightly along one stretch, and come to the junction of Trail No. 482. If you make the recommended loop you will be returning up this trail. Keep right and travel with gradual ups and downs to the junction of a spur to No. 482 at 2.8 miles. Keep straight, climb moderately through woods, make one set of switchbacks and come to a saddle where a sign states Bird Butte Summit. The actual summit, 280 feet higher, is to the west. Drop through woods for a short distance to the northeastern tip of Upper Twin Lake. Walk along the length of the eastern shore, passing several good campsites and an outbuilding, and just

before reaching the southern end pass a sign on your left marking Trail 482. If you make the recommended loop you will be following this trail on your return from Lower Twin Lake.

Keep straight and climb slightly to a point where you can look down onto a portion of the lower lake. Begin descending, switchback and continue downhill through deep woods to the junction of the Lower Twin Lakes Trail to Frog Lake Buttes. Turn left and walk downhill to the northeastern end of the lake.

To take an alternate route back to Upper Twin Lake, return to the Pacific Crest Trail and turn left. After about 150 feet be watching for an unsigned path taking off up to the right. Wind up the wooded ravine to the southern end of Upper Twin Lake, curve right and rejoin No. 2000.

To make the recommended loop, climb along No. 482, go over the crest of the ridge and traverse at a generally level grade along the east side of the slope. One-half mile from the lake pass a viewpoint just off the trail on the right then begin descending to the junction of No. 482C. Keep straight (right) and continue downhill. Come to an open crest then make a little switchback down to a meadow. Follow the markers along the eastern edge of the clearing to a sign stating Viewpoint. Turn right and traverse up the side of the low slope then curve left and climb along the broad, sparsely vegetated crest of the ridge to Palmateer Point. To complete the loop, curve left at the junction of the spur to the viewpoint and cross the meadow then begin climbing. Keep left at the junction of Trail No. 482A to Devils Half Acre and continue climbing to the Pacific Crest Trail.

Beaver pond

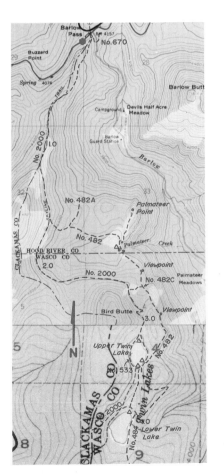

65 BARLOW BUTTE and RIDGE

One day trip
Distance: 2.7 miles one way
Elevation gain: 1,320 feet; loss 300 feet
High point: 5,069 feet
Allow 2 hours one way
Usually open late June through October
Topographic map:
  U.S.G.S. Timberline Lodge, Oreg.
  7.5'   1962

In 1845 Samuel Barlow and his small wagon train reached The Dalles and instead of waiting for rafts to take his party down the Columbia River, a costly and hazardous trip, he decided to attempt the first crossing of the Cascades by such a group. After much difficulty the party reached Oregon City and the following year he began construction of the Barlow Road. Although the trip over Barlow's toll road was exceedingly difficult, the trail became the popular access to the Willamette Valley. Naturally, several geographic features later were named for Samuel Barlow, including the landforms visited on this trip.

If you want a short hike you can make the mile long, frequently steep climb to the summit of Barlow Butte where the view includes the southeast face of Mt. Hood, Multorpor Ski Area, Devils Peak and Bird Butte across the broad valley formed by Barlow Creek. The trail continues along the crest of Barlow Ridge that extends south from the Butte. A good stopping place is a rock outcropping at the 2.7 mile point where you can see Mt. Jefferson. Carry water as none is available along the hike.

Drive on Oregon 35 to a small sign identifying the Barlow Road located 2.2 miles east of the junction of Oregon 35 and US 26 and approximately 37.8 miles south of Hood River. Continue east on Oregon 35 for 0.3 mile to a wide area along the right shoulder of the highway where a portion of the old Oregon 35 heads south. (You also can reach the trail by turning south onto Barlow Road and driving 0.2 mile to the large parking area for the Pacific Crest Trail. Walk across the road into the woods and follow the trail northeast as indicated by the sign pointing to Barlow Butte.)

From the turnout along Oregon 35 walk along the old roadbed and after 200 yards be watching for a sign below to the left stating Barlow Butte 1. Leave the road and descend for 100 yards then curve right and a few hundred feet farther come to the junction of the trail from the Pacific Crest Trail parking area. Turn south and climb moderately through woods for a short distance then begin winding up at a considerably more severe grade. Curve left along the face of the slope and where you come to a small clearing follow the path that winds up to the left for a hundred yards to the summit, the site of a former lookout tower.

To continue the hike along the ridge, return to the clearing below the summit and follow the path downhill to an open area on the ridge crest. Resume dropping then continue along or near the crest through woods and clearings, passing several large rock outcroppings. One-half mile from the junction of the short spur to Barlow Butte summit keep right where the trail forks. Climb along the slope and keep right again then travel through deeper woods. Where the trail becomes faint in a flat, open area on the crest look for the resumption of the tread at the southeast (left) edge of the clearing. Farther along at another open area on the ridge top the trail resumes at the right edge. Blazes on trees mark the route where the path is faint. At 2.5 miles begin descending to a sparsely wooded saddle where you can look ahead 50 yards to a rocky outcropping on the crest. Reenter deeper woods and traverse the north side of the slope for a short distance to an unmarked path to the right. The main trail continues to Klingers Camp. Turn right and wind up the path to the viewpoint.

Barlow Ridge from Barlow Butte

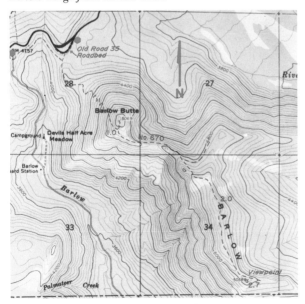

66 BOULDER LAKES

One-half day trip or backpack
Distance: 2.5 miles one way
Elevation gain: 170 feet; loss 800 feet
High point: 5,250 feet
Allow 1 to 1¼ hours one way
Usually open mid-June through October
Topographic map:
  U.S.G.S. Badger Lake, Oreg.
  7.5'   1962

Boulder Lake

Before or after the short trip to Boulder and Little Boulder Lakes you probably will want to explore the acres of grassy terrain comprising Bonney Meadows that extends to the south from the beginning of the hike. The many varieties of wild flowers scattered over the meadow are at their best during mid-June. Since the route descends to reach the lakes, you will do most of the climbing on the return trip. Begin the hike with a full bottle as the lakes do not provide satisfactory drinking water.

Proceed on Oregon 35 to Bennett Pass Road located 6.5 miles east of its junction with US 26 and 33.5 miles south of Hood River. Turn south on S21 (the Bennett Pass Road) and after 4.3 miles along the graveled surface come to the junction of S338. If you are doing the hike early in the season portions of the road ahead may be blocked by snow. However, the trailhead is only 1.4 miles farther so the extra mileage you would have to hike is not great. Keep right on S338 and after one mile continue straight at the junction of the road to the Bonney Butte helispot then 0.2 mile farther turn left at the sign marking the spur to Bonney Meadows

Campground. Go the final one-quarter mile to the beginning of the hike at a sign stating Boulder Lake Trail at the north edge of the loop through the campground.

Walk on the level and after several hundred feet come to the northernmost part of Bonney Meadows. Bonney Butte and Meadows were named for Augustus Bonney, a stockman who settled in the Tygh Valley in 1875. Cross Bonney Creek and soon enter woods. Continue at a gradual grade then curve left and begin traversing downhill. Switchback right and keep descending. The grade becomes more gradual and the trail crosses a scree slope. Reenter woods and beyond a second rocky area pass a sign at 1.5 miles identifying Kane Springs. Soon curve sharply left and begin descending at a moderately steep grade above Boulder Lake. The trail passes through a campsite along the northern shore. This is the best spot along the hike for a lunch stop or to establish a camp.

The trail continues near the shore to the exit creek and the junction of the route past tiny Spinning Lake. Keep right (straight) on the main trail and after a short distance begin climbing along a slope for 0.1 mile. At the crest descend slightly then walk on the level to within sight of shallow, tree-rimmed Little Boulder Lake. The trail tread stops before actually reaching the shore.

Bonney Creek

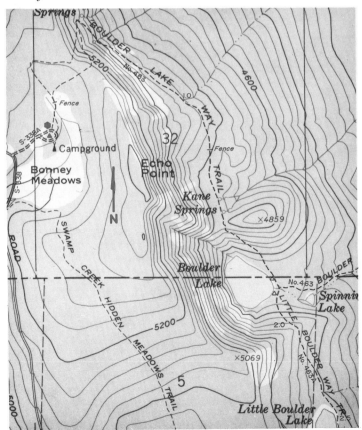

67 SERENE LAKE-CACHE MEADOW LOOP

One day trip or backpack
Distance: 7.7 miles round trip
Elevation gain: 1,910 feet; loss 1,760 feet round trip
High point: 5,000 feet
Allow 4 to 4½ hours round trip
Usually open July through October
Topographic maps:
    U.S.G.S. Fish Creek Mtn., Oreg.
    15'   **1956**
    U.S.G.S. High Rock, Oreg.
    15'   **1956**

This moderately long loop offers a variety of places to visit, each quite different in character: before reaching Serene Lake you can make two short side trips to Middle and Lower Rock Lakes and if you are doing the hike on a warm day from late July through August you may want to plan a swim in Serene Lake. The trail climbs to a viewpoint at 4.5 miles where you can look 650 feet down onto Serene Lake and north to Mounts St. Helens, Rainier, Adams and Hood then the route winds down to the grassy expanse of Cache Meadow. This is an inviting place to rest before completing the hike and the animal life in the stream at the southwest end is intriguing to observe. Except for the small stream at 1.0 mile, no potable water is available easily along the hike.

Drive 26 miles east of Estacada on the Clackamas River Road (Oregon 224) to a junction just beyond Ripplebrook Campground. Turn left onto S57 and after 7.2 miles, just beyond the bridge over Shellrock Creek, keep left on S58. At the junction of S596, 3.1 miles farther keep right following the signs to High Rock. After 3.2 miles keep left on a dirt road and 0.7 mile farther come to two roads going left. Turn left onto the upper, paved one, following the sign to High

Rock, and continue along it for 1.2 miles to an intersection. Keep left on S456 and 4.1 miles farther keep straight on S456A. Two-tenths mile from the last junction come to the Frazier Turnaround Campground where a sign marks the beginning of the Serene Lake Trail. Parking is available off the road and outhouses are near the trailhead.

Descend through woods, keeping left on the main route after a few hundred yards where an unmarked path veers off to the right. At 0.6 mile the trail passes the junction of the 0.2 mile spur to Middle Rock Lake and continues downhill for 0.1 mile to the junction of the short path that drops to Lower Rock Lake. Continue descending on the main trail to a stream crossing at 1.0 mile. Hike near a few small open areas. Descend then travel uphill and traverse along the base of an immense scree slope. Switchback up then round the face of the ridge and traverse along its northwest side before following a meandering course to the north shore of Serene Lake. Continue on the trail, cross the broad, shallow outlet creek and where the trail forks after several yards keep left. Come to the large camping area, a good spot for a rest stop, and continue to a mileage sign near an outhouse.

Traverse to the northwest up the slope then curve around the face of the ridge. Hike along the base of a scree slope then climb in switchbacks and come to a junction on a broad ridge crest. Turn left and climb moderately, keeping left (straight) at the junction of the Three Lynx Way Trail, descend slightly then resume traveling uphill to a large logged area. Continue to the east end of the clearcut, turn left, leaving the trail, and walk northwest to the rim to reach the viewpoint. The main trail begins winding downhill and at 5.2 miles comes to the northern end of Cache Meadow where the tread becomes faint then stops. Walk along the left (east) side of the clearing, go through a small strip of trees and continue along the eastern side of the meadow to a shelter in the woods at the edge of the grass. Head east from the shelter and cross a portion of the meadow, keeping a tarn on your left. Enter woods and after several yards keep left where the trail forks and begin climbing for 0.7 mile to an old road. Turn right, climb slightly then descend along the road for 1.5 miles, passing the trail to Shellrock Lake a short distance before reaching the start of the hike.

Cache Meadow

Serene Lake

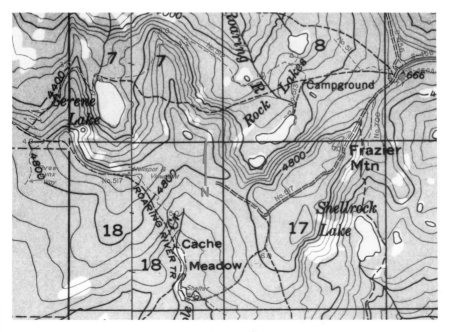

68 BAGBY HOT SPRINGS

One-half day trip
Distance: 1.5 miles one way
Elevation gain: 230 feet
High point: 2,300 feet
Allow 1 hour one way
Usually open April through November
Topographic map:
   U.S.G.S. Battle Ax, Oreg.
   15'   **1956**

At the destination of this short, easy hike through attractive woods to Bagby Hot Springs you can soak in one of the long wooden tubs in the rustic bathhouse. During mid-summer you may not even reach the Springs before getting wet since at 1.2 miles the route crosses Hot Springs Fork with many inviting pools.

If you want a longer trip you can continue south along the main trail that passes Silver King Lake after eight miles then visits Twin Lakes before ending at Elk Lake, 11 miles from the Hot Springs.

Proceed on the Clackamas River Road (Oregon 224) east of Estacada for 26 miles to a junction just beyond Ripplebrook Campground. Keep right on Oregon 224 and after several yards pass a sign indicating the mileage to Bagby Hot Springs. After 3.6 miles keep right on S63, cross the Clackamas River and continue three miles on S63 to S70. Turn right and drive five miles to Pegleg Campground. Continue on the main road 0.5 mile farther, passing Nohorn Campground, and 50 yards beyond it turn left into a large parking area where a sign near the southwest edge marks the beginning of the hike. Outbuildings are located across the clearing from the trailhead.

Several yards along the trail cross a bridge and walk near a large stream for a few hundred feet then begin climbing gradually through a scenic forest of widely spaced trees and vine maple. A section of trail along a poorly drained area has been reconstructed with planks to provide a better tread.

Traverse above the stream then veer away from the flow and come to a long, narrow footbridge. Few hikers can resist stopping along the span to peer down into the several pools. At the east end of the span curve right and climb a short distance. An unsigned trail that heads uphill to your left originally went to Pansy Basin but now the route ends in a clearcut. Just beyond the junction cross a small footbridge and climb the final 0.1 mile to the Bagby Guard Station. The bathhouse is down the slope to the north of the station and a creek flows just below the bathhouse. The Springs were named for Robert W. Bagby, a prospector and miner who once worked the area.

Bridge over Hot Springs Fork (above) Bagby Hot Springs bath house (below)

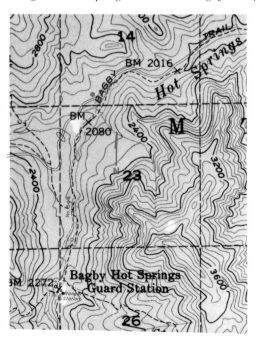

155

69 PANSY BASIN and BULL OF THE WOODS

One day trip
Distance: 3.6 miles one way
Elevation gain: 2,150 feet
High point: 5,523 feet
Allow 2 to 2½ hours one way
Usually open late June through mid-November
Topographic map:
    U.S.G.S. Battle Ax, Oreg.
    15'   1956

Bull of the Woods Lookout

Bull of the Woods is the most southerly summit described in this guide and it affords views of the main peaks in the Central Oregon Cascades — Mt. Jefferson, the spires of Three Fingered Jack and Mt. Washington and the clustered Three Sisters in addition to Mounts Hood, St. Helens, Rainier and Adams to the north. A few short portions of the climb are steep but, overall, the trail follows a moderate grade. You can do the return trip as a loop that involves no elevation gain and very little additional mileage.

Drive east of Estacada 26 miles on the Clackamas River Road (Oregon 224) to a junction just beyond Ripplebrook Campground. Keep right on Oregon 224 then after 3.6 miles keep right on S63 and continue on S63 for 5.5 miles to the junction with S708 and turn right, leaving the paved road, onto an oiled surface. After 7.7 miles keep right, following the sign pointing to Pansy Basin Trail, and 3.5 miles farther come to a sign on your left marking the beginning of the Pansy Basin Trail. Parking spaces are available along the shoulders of the road.

Walk through woods for a short distance then drop slightly into a sink hole. Cross the open area on a rocky trail then reenter deep woods. Climb gradually then more steeply before leveling off and descending briefly to a stream crossing at 0.8 mile. This is the last good source of water along the hike. Several yards beyond the flow come to the junction of the trail you will be following if you make the described loop.

Keep straight (right) and after several yards drop slightly into a meadow where an abundance of wild flowers bloom during mid-summer. Where the trail forks keep right and continue across the clearing. Near the west edge of the meadow curve left and begin rising moderately through a rocky, semi-open area. Enter woods and begin climbing steeply then level off and pass near the east shore of a pond. Continue at a gradual grade to a shelter. Pansy Lake, not visible from the campground, is about 100 feet downslope.

Continue along the trail that heads southwest from the shelter and begin climbing. Come to an open area at an old mine shaft where you can see down onto Pansy Lake and across upper Pansy Basin to the lookout tower on the summit of Bull of the Woods. Soon begin dropping and where a faint path heads south keep left on the main trail. Descend toward the lake for a short distance then curve sharply right and climb very steeply to a saddle at 1.9 miles and the junction of the Mother Lode Trail.

Turn left, traverse uphill and 0.3 mile from the saddle make a short set of switchbacks then continue traversing the wooded slope. Pass through a grassy patch and come to the junction of the Welcome Lake Trail (No. 70) just below the ridge crest. Turn left and traverse at a gradual grade for 0.3 mile then switchback right. After a brief traverse make three short switchbacks and come to the open summit area.

To make the loop continue along the trail below the tower and descend to the north along the west side of the ridge. Enter woods and continue downhill along the crest before making two sets of short switchbacks and traversing two grassy clearings. Go through a small burn before coming to a junction one mile from the lookout, turn left and continue dropping. Walk through an open area then pass above a large pond and wind down the final distance to the junction with the trail you followed on the way up.

Big Slide Lake

70 WELCOME LAKES

One day trip or backpack
Distance: 5 miles one way
Elevation gain: 2,000 feet; loss 200 feet
High point: 4,400 feet
Allow 2 hours one way
Usually open June through October
Topographic map:
   U.S.G.S. Battle Ax, Oreg.
    15'   1956

Indian Pond Lily

The climb to Welcome Lakes is the most southerly of the hikes described in this guide and you can enjoy more of the area by making a two mile loop above West Welcome Lake. With a little more effort you could continue another mile to the summit of Bull of the Woods (No. 69) that affords views of the major peaks from the Three Sisters north to Mt. Rainier. Trails also go to other landmarks in the area such as Big Slide Lake and Schreiner Paek. In August delicious red huckleberries are abundant between 1.0 and 2.0 miles.

Proceed on the Clackamas River Road (Oregon 224) east of Estacada 26 miles to a junction just beyond Ripplebrook Campground. Keep right on Oregon 224 then after 3.6 miles keep right on S63 and continue on it for 14.7 miles to a bridge. Cross the span, turn right onto S820 and drive 0.5 mile to a clearcut and a sign stating Elk Lake Trail. Parking is available a few yards up the road.

After a few feet pass a sign listing several mileages and continue one-quarter mile through the clearcut to its western edge. Traverse along a wooded slope, drop slightly along the sometimes rocky trail and resume climbing. Descend into the little side canyon formed by Pine Cone Creek, cross the flow and continue through woods. At 1.5 miles keep right at an old grey sign that marks the junction of the faint Janus Butte and East Fork Trails and travel at a gradual grade then descend to the crossing of Knob Rock Creek. Several feet farther ford a second flow, the last plentiful source of water along the hike, and climb to the junction of the trail that goes south to Battle Creek shelter. Stay right and begin a series of moderately steep switchbacks. The trail traverses along a valley wall high above Welcome Creek and near 4.0 miles the grade becomes more gradual. Cross the base of a brush-rimmed scree slope, hop a small stream and just beyond it pass an unmarked trail that descends to the lowest and largest of the Welcome Lakes.

Keep left on the main trail and climb for 0.2 mile to a large, dry campsite at the junction of the path to Upper Welcome Lake. Turn right and walk a few hundred feet to the lake that in late summer is covered with yellow pond lily blossoms. From the viewpoint to the east of the lake you can look 200 feet down onto the lowest Welcome Lake.

For the suggested loop, return to the main trail and climb in short switchbacks through more open terrain to the junction of the Geronimo Trail. Turn right and travel near the crest to the Schreiner Peak Trail. To reach Bull of the Woods keep left, continue near the crest, keep right at the next junction and continue the final 0.4 mile to the summit. For the shorter loop, turn right at the junction of the Schreiner Peak Trail and descend in very short, moderately steep switchbacks to the junction of the Dickey Creek Trail to Big Slide Lake. Turn right, continuing on the Schreiner Peak Trail, and after a few yards pass a pond. Cross a saddle and come to the junction of West Lake Way. Turn right and descend slightly 250 feet above West Welcome Lake. Traverse at a gradual grade and three-quarters mile from the Schreiner Peak Trail round a corner and descend to the northeastern shore of Upper Welcome Lake.

Falls on West Welcome Creek

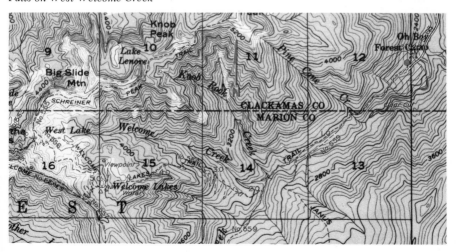

Cover Photo, Ramona Falls

Photo Page 9, Mt. Hood from the summit of
          Lost Lake Butte

Cover Design, Robert Reynolds

Editor, Thomas K. Worcester